Undivided Witness is a must read for those who are serious about community development, transformation and vibrant communities of Jesus followers coming into being. It does a brilliant job in laying a biblical and theological foundation for community development, as well as in sharing critical principles to greatly assist those who serve the relevant communities. What I especially like about the book is that it draws on the experience and expertise of practitioners as it seeks to highlight issues such as the Kingdom of God, best practice and what it means to take the shalom of God to the least reached. It is so refreshing to hear a polyphonic symphony of voices from around the world running throughout Undivided Witness.

Peter Tarantal, Associate International Director, OM;
Chair, World Evangelical Alliance Mission Commission

The practical examples shared throughout this book ground its teaching in reality, helping us apply what we read to our everyday ministry. At the heart of all our witness is a love that compels us to serve in word and deed, in season and out of season. This book brings theology and practice together and enables us to live out an undivided witness. The wealth of experience expressed throughout makes you hunger for more and to become more engaged oneself. I highly recommend *Undivided Witness* as a key resource for all of us to draw from.

Sheryl Haw, theologian and aid practitioner;
former International Director for Micah Global/Micah Network.

Many churches now fly the flag of 'Integral Mission', but often this simply means moving into poor communities and using community development or some such intervention as a platform for evangelism. Mission groups and development organisations in hard places find themselves in tension between 'church planting' and the demands of 'Kingdom witness'. This book is a good start in exploring from the ground up the paradigm shifts needed so that community engagement becomes truly missional. The stories give flesh to the seamlessness of 'undivided witness', how sensitive and disinterested acts of compassion paradoxically lead to spiritual curiosity, and the consequent formation of Jesus followers in restricted contexts. This is a valuable keepsake in the journey towards transformation, not just of communities, but of practitioners themselves.

Melba Padilla Maggay, Founder,
Institute for Studies in Asian Church and Culture (ISACC)

The Church over the years has meandered in its search to find ways to respond to what the 1966 Berlin Congress identified as 'inadequacies in the human race.' In the process, we experimented with community development, Christian development, transformational development, wholistic development, integral development—and the journey continues. *Undivided Witness* takes an interesting step forward to identify a 'credible integrator'—using various theological motifs like the Kingdom of God, grace, salvation, and redemption—as it explores the space between 'community development, the least reached, and vibrant communities of Jesus followers'. The book also provides key principles to operationalise this 'space' into real life and address difficult issues that grassroots frontliners encounter. *Undivided Witness* is an asset for those involved in community development as an act of obedience to the call of God in their lives.

Dr. Jayakumar Christian, former National Director,
World Vision India and Vice-President for
Faith and Development, World Vision International

UNDIVIDED WITNESS

June 15, 2024

Dearest Imee, Dodong, Trent & Luke,

Thanks for having us — such a joy to be here! May God continue to bless you all as you truly been a real channel of blessings to many!

In His witness,
Ate Sally

Regnum Series Preface

While we delight to serve the academic community, our mission is to enable the global church to engage more readily in God's mission in its very diverse contexts. To do this we seek to bring practitioners and academics together. Our desire is that this series will bridge the gap that sometimes exists between, on the one hand, Christian leaders and mission practitioners and, on the other, Christian researchers.

About the Editors

David Greenlee (PhD), raised in Colombia, is Operation Mobilisation's Director of Missiological Research and Evaluation.

Mark Galpin (PhD) has 30 years' experience in community development in South Asia and Africa and is the Postgraduate Programme Leader at All Nations Christian College.

Paul Bendor-Samuel (MD) is Executive Director of the Oxford Centre for Mission Studies and past International Director of Interserve.

UNDIVIDED WITNESS:
FOLLOWERS OF JESUS, COMMUNITY DEVELOPMENT, AND LEAST-REACHED COMMUNITIES

David Greenlee, Mark Galpin,
and Paul Bendor-Samuel (eds)

Copyright © David Greenlee 2020

First published 2020 by Regnum Books International

Regnum is an imprint of the Oxford Centre for Mission Studies
St. Philip and St. James Church, Woodstock Road, Oxford, OX2 6HR, UK
www.ocms.ac.uk/regnum

09 08 07 06 05 04 03 8 7 6 5 4 3 2 1

The right of David Greenlee, Mark Galpin, and Paul Bendor-Samuel to be identified as the editors of this work have been asserted by him in accordance with the Copyright, Designs and Patents Act 1988.

All rights reserved. No part of this publication may be reproduced, stored in a retrieval system, or transmitted, in any form or by any means, electronic, mechanical, photocopying, recording or otherwise, without the prior permission of the publisher or a license permitting restricted copying. In the UK such licenses are issued by the Copyright Licensing Agency, 90 Tottenham Court Road, London W1P 9HE.

Unless otherwise indicated, Scripture taken from the *Holy Bible*, NEW INTERNATIONAL VERSION®, NIV® Copyright © 1973, 1978, 1984, 2011 by Biblica, Inc.® Used by permission. All rights reserved worldwide.

Scripture quotations marked NLT are taken from the *Holy Bible*, New Living Translation, copyright © 1996, 2004, 2007. Used by permission of Tyndale House Publishers, Inc., Carol Stream, Illinois 60188. All rights reserved.

Scripture quotations marked JB are taken from *The Jerusalem Bible* © 1966 by Darton, Longman & Todd Ltd. and Doubleday and Company Ltd.

British Library Cataloguing in Publication Data
A catalogue record for this book is available from the British Library

ISBN: 978-1-5064-8374-0

eBook ISBN: 978-1-5064-8396-2

Typeset in Palatino by WORDS BY DESIGN

Cover photograph © Quang Nguyen Minh from pixabay.com

Distributed by 1517 Media in the US, Canada, India, and Brazil

DEDICATION

We thought we had left home to serve
  But so often you have served us.
We came to you, often thinking we had something to teach
  But discovered we had so much to learn.
We often thought you were 'least-reached' and far away
  Then began to see the barriers in our own hearts.
We set off compelled by love
  And have been warmed by the love we together have shared.
We walk this path because we follow Jesus
  And rejoice that some of you now follow him as well.

You have welcomed us into your lives, your homes, and your communities
  In Himalayan mountains and Central Asian valleys
  On the coast of Indian Ocean islands and shores of African lakes
  In the **barangays** *of Filipino cities*
    and the housing estates of England's North

To you we dedicate this book: our friends, neighbours, and teachers.

Contents

Introduction: exploring a new space in missiology and community development
Mark Galpin and David Greenlee — 1

The Ten CDLR Principles — 15

1. Principle 1:
Understanding the Kingdom of God is fundamental
Jonathan Williams — 21

2. Principle 2:
Understanding how people enter the Kingdom of God shapes how we do ministry
David Greenlee — 33

3. Principle 3:
The gospel impacts the whole person and people's whole contexts
Rizalina (Sally) Ababa — 43

4. Principle 4:
A broad vision of glorifying Christ
Gabriel (Gabby) Markus — 55

Reflection: Ethical evangelism: integrity, truth timing, and grace
Mark Galpin — 65

5. Principle 5:
Prayer, spiritual warfare, and change
Holly Steward — 71

6. Principle 6:
Caring for creation as worship, witness, and obedience
Robert Sluka — 83

7. Principle 7:
   A vision for renewal and vibrant communities
      of Jesus followers
   Mark Galpin   97

8. Principle 8:
   Community development workers are committed
      to professional excellence
   Scott Breslin   109

   Reflection: Corruption, community development,
      and the least reached
   Martin Allaby   123

9. Principle 9:
   Shared principles of excellence
   Andrea C. Waldorf   131

10. Principle 10:
    The least reached are so for a reason
    Rosemary Hack   143

    Reflection: Serving the least reached through community
       development: a personal journey of understanding
    A community development worker in Asia   157

    Epilogue: Called to undivided witness
    Paul Bendor-Samuel   163

    Contributors   169
    For Further Reading   171
    General Index   177
    Scripture Index   183

Introduction: Exploring a New Space

Mark Galpin and David Greenlee

Embodied Love

> In 2014 our team started praying about moving into one of the most conservative, least-reached towns in our Central Asian, post-Soviet, Muslim country. Soon, our agency received what we considered to be our 'Macedonian call': an invitation from the mayor and leaders of the local association of the blind and visually impaired to engage in water and other projects in this district.
>
> As we moved into the city, our team of expatriate workers, highly trained in community development as well as cultural relevance, experienced a welcoming spirit of hospitality. Local townsfolk told us of supernatural signs they experienced, such as dreams about welcoming us because we would do good things. One of us reached out to the community concerning the situation of children with disabilities. The worker openly prayed with workers of the Muslim partner organisation for a lead on how to find the children. Within minutes, a government social worker entered the room and asked for help in their work.
>
> By 2018 the project was serving 200 families and children with disabilities. The interventions range from basic rehabilitation and production of assistive devices to training parents and social workers on the causes of disabilities. In that training we counter folk beliefs that the children are cursed or punished by God. Speaking about our creation in the image of God opens ways to share stories of Jesus. In turn, several of the women have engaged in Discovery Bible Studies in the last year. I would call what we have here a 'vibrant group of Jesus seekers'. They are starting to be transformed as they move closer and closer to him and are already transforming their communities by acting out his commandments.
>
> *A long-term development worker in Central Asia*

People being drawn to Jesus through the changed lives and loving behaviour of Christians is not a 21st-century missiological innovation. Alan Kreider observes that changed lives were the key to growth of the Church in the third and fourth centuries. 'What the outsiders saw was not their worship. It was their habitus',[1] the kind of 'good lives among the pagans' that caused them to glorify God (1 Pet. 2:12) and recognise that they were Jesus' disciples (John 13:34–35). Kreider continues:

> According to Tertullian, the outsiders looked at the Christians and saw them energetically feeding poor people and burying them, caring for boys and girls who lacked property and parents, and being attentive to aged slaves and prisoners. They interpreted these actions as a 'work of love.' And they said 'Vide, look! How they love one another.' [Tertullian, Apology 39.7] They did not say 'Aude, listen to the Christians' message'; they did not say, 'Lege, read what they write.' Hearing and reading were important, and some early Christians worked to communicate in these ways too. But we must not miss the reality: the pagans said look! Christianity's truth was visible; it was embodied and enacted by its members. It was made tangible, sacramental.[2]

FOCUS

Much has been learned and many volumes published concerning the planting, formation and growth of churches. This has been accompanied by research into 'unreached people groups' and 'the unevangelised'; many mission agencies have made church planting and evangelism among these groups the focus of their mission goals and strategies.

Community development and the alleviation of poverty and suffering has been a key focus of other organisations, particularly Christian faith-based relief and development agencies. More recently, these themes have been increasingly studied in depth by missiologists with a growing interest in evangelical circles in what Bryant Myers termed 'transformational development' in the 1999 first edition of his benchmark work *Walking with the Poor*.[3]

In practice, a number of mission organisations focusing on evangelism and church planting among the least reached have included aspects of community development in their work, though often not as a mainstream activity. Meanwhile, those organisations focused on community development have often found that their work with communities leads to people coming to faith in Jesus Christ and, at times, the emergence of fledgling churches. While this has happened in practice, and is a phenomenon familiar to practitioners, rarely have missiologists explored the overlap between these domains. Indeed, often the respective disciplines of

Introduction

church planting and community development have been treated as being in tension or competition with each other rather than as areas of potential fruitful synergy with many principles of good practice in common.

The contributors to this book address this gap by exploring the conceptual and practical intersection between community development, the least reached, and the emergence of vibrant, growing churches or 'communities of Jesus followers' that we refer to as the 'Community Development Least Reached' (CDLR) space. While the principles we explore overlap with other spaces, our intention is to shed light on an area familiar to some practitioners but left largely untouched in published missiology. One exception is the recent doctoral research by Christian Giordano who examined the relationship between the implementation of development projects by evangelical, Iberoamerican missionaries (that is, from Latin America, Spain, and Portugal) and the emergence of new communities of Jesus followers in Muslim contexts in North Africa, Senegal, and Uzbekistan.[4]

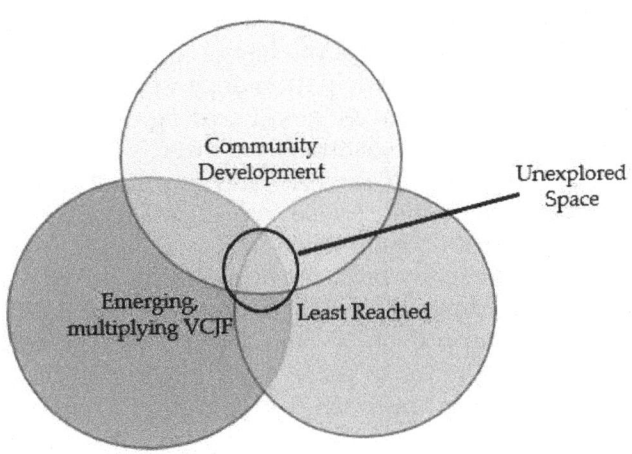

The unexplored CDLR space

DEFINITIONS

Before going further it is important that we briefly define the three phrases we use to describe the focus of the 'CDLR space' explored by the contributors to this book.

Community development and relief:

For the purposes of this discussion we will use the term 'community development' (CD) in its widest sense. We define community development as a long-term process in which 'community members come together to take collective action and generate solutions to common problems'.[5, 6] The term encompasses a variety of approaches from more sector-focused projects in which outputs are clearly defined, to more process-focused approaches with broader, more interdisciplinary impact.

Among Christian agencies, approaches emphasising the 'incarnational presence' of CD workers living in the community have also been accentuated. More recently, strength-based approaches to community development have gained popularity and credence. While these approaches differ, all seek to draw on the knowledge, experience, and resources of community members to engage them in a process of change to achieve their desired goals. While the levels of participation depend on the approach used, this inclusiveness is seen as key in bringing about empowerment, leading to long-term sustainable change.

Within contexts of poverty and marginalisation, people's lives are often punctuated by severe crises requiring the short-term provision of resources to meet basic needs and avoid further loss of life. These crises may be at the household level or community-wide, such as the impact of a natural disaster. While community development approaches often seek to reduce vulnerabilities and strengthen resilience to these risks, in the face of crisis, short-term provision or relief approaches are required to enable the community to survive. These 'relief' interventions are often followed by a phase of 'rehabilitation' where a community is assisted to return to the standard of living they had prior to the disaster. While conceptually a clear boundary is often drawn between relief, rehabilitation, and (community) development, it is now recognised that in practice there is a much more dynamic relationship between these phases of intervention. Effective relief and rehabilitation incorporate

Introduction

community development principles such as empowerment and participation. Organisations working in contexts of poverty often must switch from longer-term community development approaches to the provision of lifesaving relief in the wake of disasters and back again. For this book, our definition of community development therefore includes all of these phases and incorporates stories and case studies from each of these phases of intervention.

We recognise that the practice and implementation of community development often overlaps with many other disciplines, approaches, and ministry areas. These might include enterprise development and business, sports ministry, the arts, education, and political involvement, among others. The boundaries between what we term community development and these approaches are not always clear. CD may incorporate or lead to these other areas and can also be a result of these other areas of involvement. Our focus on CD in this study is not intended to treat other approaches as irrelevant but to give an adequate focus and boundary to our study and reflection. The principles discussed in this book may well be relevant to these related ministry areas, and we welcome and encourage reflection on this to build on the work in this book.

'Least reached':
In this book our focus is on community development with and among the 'least reached'. By this term we mean communities among whom:
   a. There has been no gospel engagement. No one is living, proclaiming, and demonstrating the gospel among them, nor has there been a positive response to God's grace in all its truth; or
   b. There has been gospel engagement, but no gospel-centred and gospel-proclaiming community of Jesus followers is present; or
   c. There is a community of Jesus followers living, proclaiming, and demonstrating the gospel but, due to geographical distance, cultural barriers or linguistic obstacles, access to it is significantly limited for the vast majority of that people or community.[7]

We have intentionally used the term 'least reached' rather than 'unreached' due to the associated idea of 'unreached people groups', which emphasises clearly defined ethnolinguistic groups. While in some settings community development is carried out with specific ethnolinguistic groups, more often our work includes people from a range of 'people groups', who are unified by their experience of poverty or marginalisation whether through disability, disease, or disaster. Our CD work therefore focuses on all of those affected by these issues, independent of their ethnolinguistic or religious identity.

'Vibrant Communities of Jesus Followers (VCJF)':
Our interest is in examining the phenomenon of churches that emerge among the least reached through community development work. The term 'church' has at times become laden with unhelpful meanings related to buildings and structures and is often weighed down with historical baggage which can be particularly problematic in least-reached, restrictive settings. We therefore use the term 'vibrant communities of Jesus followers' (VCJF), pointing back to the biblical model of *ekklesia*. This terminology is particularly helpful in restrictive contexts where followers of Jesus might identify themselves by their relationship with Jesus rather than with words such as 'Christians' or as a 'church'.

EXPLORING A NEW SPACE
Our motivation for this study grew out of the desire of community development workers serving with Operation Mobilisation (OM) and its partners to better align ourselves with and identify our contribution to OM's shared vision 'to see vibrant communities of Jesus followers among the least reached'. In working to clarify our own principles and shared understandings, we realised that while Christian community development practitioners within OM and beyond have gained significant experience in this area very little has been written or formally researched to explore the CDLR space.

Within evangelical development circles there has, in the last two decades, been an increased recognition and focus on engaging the local church, with significant movements of local churches playing a central role in bringing transformative change to their local communities. However, our focus by definition is on areas where the local church is yet to become established and existing contact with the church is limited. When we extend our thinking to least-reached settings, the questions—and possibly the answers—are

Introduction

different from past research based on areas where churches and Christians are well-established. While there are some (previously) least-reached settings where many have turned quickly to faith in Jesus Christ, questions of timing and patience are required both in terms of community change in general as well as in terms of a positive response to the good news. And while some have explored the role of the church where it is already an accepted part of society,[8] what is our role where there is no (or very little) local expression of the church? What should our contribution be, given that not all—and perhaps very few—of the local community will come to faith in Jesus Christ any time soon, even if we long for a rapid movement of people turning to him?

In a conversation between David Greenlee and Bryant Myers in June 2018, Myers confirmed what he had previously observed in print,[9] that while there is an increasing interest in what Myers first called 'transformational development',[10] still very little has been researched or published on the CDLR space.[11] Myers writes that Bob Mitchell offers 'the first systematic field-based academic research on the theory and practices of faith-based development done by a Christian organization'.[12] Interacting with Mitchell is vitally important. We share his concerns about inappropriate, programmatic evangelism linked to community development work;[13] however, we would more intentionally incorporate into our principles and work a desire not just for transformed, vibrant communities but also for the establishment of vibrant communities of Jesus followers.

The ten principles that form the basis for the chapters of this book were first developed at a meeting hosted by the Oxford Centre for Mission Studies in October 2018. Six OM workers with significant experience in community development were joined by an OM missiologist, faculty experienced in development work at OCMS and All Nations Christian College, and a colleague from another agency. The principles were distilled from the group's shared understandings and reflections and later refined through an extended online discussion among selected OM workers and partners in other agencies. These were then published in the journal *Transformation* in 2019.[14]

This approach of corporate reflection and drawing principles from experience is valid for a number of reasons, including:

- the familiarity of the contributors with the issues, given they have spent many years embedded in the communities they serve
- the range of ministries they have participated in and that are included in the broad domain of community development
- the geographic spread of cases, which includes different parts of South Asia, Southeast Asia, Central Asia, the Middle East, and Africa, and among refugees in Europe
- the communal nature of the process that enables shared learning.

In this book, the contributors expand on each of the principles identified in that paper, exploring in more depth both the theory and thinking behind these principles and how they work out in practice. Our intention is not to provide an instructive 'how to' manual nor to produce a purely academic text but to share both the experience of working in this CDLR space from a range of different regions and organisations and the theory behind the work undertaken in these areas. We have drawn on a diverse range of authors, all with significant experience in this over-arching area of ministry but in very diverse geographical, cultural, and ministry contexts. We have sought to ensure that their individual voices can be heard and their stories told; through them we can hear the voices of those we serve. Individual chapters will therefore have differing styles with some being more personal and practical and others delving more into theology and theory. In addition, while each chapter focuses on one of the ten principles developed, we recognise that these principles do not operate in isolation from each other; they interact, synergise, and build upon each other. While we have attempted to minimise any unnecessary repetition, our hope is that the interrelatedness of the principles comes across in the book as a whole.

WHERE OUR STUDY FITS

Both secular and Christian approaches to community development recognise that poverty is complex and multidimensional and that effective development approaches must facilitate communities to move out of poverty in multiple dimensions. Indian economist and philosopher Amartya Sen describes development as 'a process of expanding the real freedoms that people enjoy' and postulates that 'the enhancement of human freedom is both the main object and the

Introduction

primary means of development', reminding us that poverty and development are not merely financial or technological issues.[15]

Christian development thinkers also emphasise the holistic nature of change that is required for effective transformation. Myers suggests that the goal of Christian development is 'restored relationships' or *shalom* and highlights the importance of aligning the community's story with God's story.[16]

The biblical story starts with a picture of *shalom* in the garden of Eden with Adam and Eve living in perfect harmony with themselves, each other, creation, and God. Their disobedience results in the breaking of all these relationships by sin. They hide from God when he comes walking in the garden, as they see themselves naked and experience shame—a broken relationship with self. Adam accuses Eve and then God for their disobedience, and part of the punishment for Eve is that her husband will rule over her. Adam's punishment is that work becomes hard and burdensome as God curses the earth. Adam and Eve are then banished from the garden.

The story of the fall is a 'holistic mess' resulting in psychological, social, spiritual, and ecological brokenness.[17] The rest of the biblical story is of how God goes about restoring that *shalom*, ultimately through the life, death, and resurrection of Jesus. The vertical spiritual relationship between God and humanity, broken by sin, is restored as we, who are in Christ, are reconciled to God (2 Cor. 5:18). The horizontal social relationships between different parts of humanity are restored as all are made one in Christ Jesus (Eph. 2:14–18). The psychological relationship with self is restored as we no longer bear the guilt and shame of sin but are made righteous through Christ (Rom. 5:19), and the cosmic and ecological nature of redemption is revealed as all things in heaven and earth are reconciled to God in Christ (Col. 1:15–20).

At the end of the biblical story, expanding on pictures only partially seen in the Old Testament prophets, in Revelation 21 and 22 we are given a picture of the new heavens and the new earth. *Shalom* is once more restored; there is no more crying, weeping, pain, or death (Rev. 21:4). The curse is removed from the earth, and God dwells once more with his people, who are from every tribe and every nation. The corollary of the Hebrew concept of *shalom* in the New Testament is the idea of 'fullness of life' (John 10:10), often used in the vision statements of Christian relief and development agencies and which in some cases has been taken further to specifically impact practice.[18]

The biblical story is a living story, a story we are part of.[19] Understanding the current stage of the story—where we live between the first and the second coming of Christ, where God's Kingdom has been inaugurated but has not yet come to completion—is vital for our praxis.

AN OVERVIEW OF THE CHAPTERS

We open the book with a list of our ten CDLR principles followed by a chapter corresponding to each principle. These chapters are linked by three reflection essays that draw on themes linking the principles.

Beginning the discussion in Chapter 1, Jonathan Williams explores the principle that understanding the Kingdom of God is crucial to understanding the link between community development and the emergence of VCJF. In Chapter 2, David Greenlee discusses how we enter the Kingdom and the principle that how we understand the way people enter the Kingdom impacts how we go about ministry.

Drawing on her extensive experience in the Philippines, in Chapter 3 Rizalina 'Sally' Ababa explores the idea of integral mission: not a programme or list of activities but a life-long intentional commitment emanating from our hearts that involves our whole being and all that we say and do. An understanding of the Kingdom, and of God's *shalom*-restoring agenda, means that while we long for individuals to come to faith in Christ, our vision does not stop there. We want to see the Kingdom of God impact the communities and societies where we live and serve. Gabriel Markus, who has coordinated responses in post-tsunami Sri Lanka and during the 2015 refugee crisis in Greece, explores this principle in Chapter 4 and addresses the issue of our response when we do not see visible spiritual fruit. Mark Galpin then draws our focus to issues of 'ethical evangelism' in the first reflection essay. Presenting the message of God's grace is not unethical, but how we go about it might be, which is why understanding God's Kingdom and the context are important.

Transformation in the Christian sense does not take place without spiritual conflict. In Chapter 5 Holly Steward reflects on her years

Introduction

serving in Zambia to explore this principle. Robert Sluka, a marine biologist who leads A Rocha's Marine and Coastal Conservation Programme, explores in Chapter 6 the overlap between community development and creation care. Creation care is not simply a principle that helps us achieve the aims expressed in the CDLR process, but a goal at the heart of the paradigm.

While both secular and Christian approaches to community development recognise the need for change and freedom in multiple areas of life and society, biblically faithful approaches to community development must include the opportunity for community members to experience 'freedom in Christ' and put their faith in Jesus and become a part of 'vibrant communities of Jesus followers'. *Shalom* or 'fullness of life' cannot be experienced without a restored relationship with God through Christ; we cannot talk of 'transformation' without this inner transformation of the heart. These principles are taken up specifically in Chapter 7 by Mark Galpin.

Galpin's concerns flow naturally into the theme of Chapter 8 in which Scott Breslin, with many years' experience directing a community development-focused NGO, emphasises the important principle of upholding ethical and professional standards in our work. Corruption is an issue of global concern, a factor reinforcing the power of poverty and a thread running through several of our principles. Martin Allaby's reflection on this theme offers biblical and historical insights to help us respond to corruption in least-reached settings.

In Chapter 9 Andrea Waldorf compares synergies and commonalities between principles of good community development practice and effective church planting approaches.

To conclude our exploration of the ten principles, in Chapter 10 Rosemary Hack examines the multiple reasons that people are 'least reached'. Identifying and reaching them involves intentional effort; our own blurred vision, biases, and even our comfort may prevent us from recognising and serving them. To remind us that we are not discussing merely theoretical professional or missiological concepts, our final reflection comes from the heart of a colleague (unnamed out of privacy concerns) who recounts her journey among the 'least reached' from South African townships near her own home to jungles of Southeast Asia and mountains of Central Asia.

Paul Bendor-Samuel then concludes our book, noting important questions and pointing to what might come next. His thoughts are important markers as we move ahead, in particular his reminder of the need to not just listen to our own voices, but to do the harder work of listening to the communities God is calling us to serve.

OUR HOPES FOR THIS BOOK

Our overall hope and aim in writing this book is that it will stimulate more reflection and discussion on this area of ministry, contribute to a rarely explored theme in missiology, and encourage the discovery and recognition of the links between community development and the emergence of 'vibrant communities of Jesus followers' in least-reached settings. By demonstrating the synergy between church planting and community development, we hope to dissolve the perceived tension between these ministry approaches and to encourage organisations that have traditionally focused on church planting and evangelism to recognise the strategic role community development can play in achieving their Kingdom objectives in least-reached contexts—never to be used merely as a platform but as an integral feature of truly holistic mission.

In addition, we hope that our work will influence and shape the practice of those already committed to the strategy of community development as a ministry approach in least-reached contexts, enabling them to become more effective and transformative in building God's Kingdom.

While we have confidence in these principles, we consider them to still be under development. Input from readers is therefore welcome to both refine the principles and to develop a robust explanation and grounding for each. In turn, this will help us contribute to a missiology that guides ministry and service involving community development among the least reached.

A NOTE ON STYLE AND REFERENCING

At times specific individuals are named. If the first time a name is used it employs a highlighted font with an asterisk following (*David**) that indicates the name has been changed out of privacy concerns. We seek to supply ample references to point to our sources rather than burdening the text with unnecessary detail. We build our work on the writing of many others.

Introduction

Finally, together with the chapter authors we express thanks to our fellow editor Paul Bendor-Samuel and his colleagues at the Oxford Centre for Mission Studies. They hosted the October 2018 consultation that gave rise to this volume and have encouraged us in ongoing work related to this theme. Thanks also to the Regnum Books staff for their help in moving the publication forward and to Tony Gray of Words by Design who helped us turn the manuscript into the book you are now reading. Finally, we acknowledge the editorial contribution of Greg Kernaghan who helped us express our thoughts in what we hope is both clear and reasonably concise form.

ENDNOTES

---

[1] Alan Kreider, *The Patient Ferment of the Early Church: The Improbable Rise of Christianity in the Roman Empire* (Grand Rapids: Baker Academic, 2016), 61.

[2] Kreider, 61.

[3] Bryant L. Myers, *Walking with the Poor: Principles and Practices of Transformational Development* (Maryknoll: Orbis, 1999).

[4] Christian Giordano Quintana, 'En busca de una misiología integral: las relaciones entre proyectos de desarrollo iberoamericanos no proselitistas en tierras musulmanas y las iglesias pioneras vinculadas a ellos' (PhD dissertation, Amsterdam, Vrije Universiteit, 2020), https://research.vu.nl/ws/portalfiles/portal/96812765/356685.pdf.

[5] 'Community Development', UNTERM: The United Nations Terminology Database, 3 June 2019, https://unterm.un.org.

[6] 'What Is Community Development?', Community Development Exchange, 14 July 2010, https://web.archive.org/web/20100714160130/http://www.cdx.org.uk/community-development/what-community-development.

[7] Operation Mobilisation, 'Moving toward Seeing Vibrant Communities of Jesus Followers among the Least Reached', January 2017.

[8] Sebastian C. H. Kim, *Theology in the Public Sphere: Public Theology as a Catalyst for Open Debate* (London: SCM Press, 2011).

[9] Bryant L. Myers, 'Holistic Mission: New Frontiers', in Brian Woolnough and Wonsuk Ma (eds), *Holistic Mission: God's Plan for God's People* (Oxford: Regnum, 2010), 119–27; Bryant L. Myers, 'Foreword: Expanding Our Horizons', in Bob Mitchell, *Faith-Based Development: How Christian Organizations Can Make a Difference* (Maryknoll: Orbis, 2017), ix–xii.
[10] Myers, *Walking with the Poor*, 1999.
[11] David Greenlee, Personal conversation, Bryant Myers with David Greenlee, June 2018.
[12] Myers, 'Foreword', x.
[13] Mitchell, *Faith-Based Development*, 2017, 38, 95.
[14] David Greenlee et al., 'Exploring the Intersection of Community Development, the Least Reached, and Emerging, Vibrant Churches', *Transformation* 37.2 (April 2020), 105-118, https://doi.org/10.1177/0265378819886223.
[15] Amartya Sen, *Development as Freedom* (Oxford: Oxford University Press, 2001), 3.
[16] Bryant L. Myers, *Walking with the Poor: Principles and Practices of Transformational Development*, Rev. ed. (Maryknoll: Orbis, 2011), 96–97.
[17] Christopher J. H. Wright, *The Mission of God: Unlocking the Bible's Grand Narrative* (Downers Grove: IVP Academic, 2006), 315.
[18] Mark Galpin, 'Moving from Vision to Practice: Making Fullness of Life Practical' (Lima, Peru: 6th Global Consultation of Micah Global, 2015).
[19] Mark Galpin, *Living in God's Story: Understanding the Bible's Grand Narrative* (United Kingdom: Micah im:press, 2018).

TEN PRINCIPLES RELATING COMMUNITY DEVELOPMENT, THE LEAST REACHED, AND VIBRANT COMMUNITIES OF JESUS FOLLOWERS

1. Understanding the Kingdom of God is crucial to understanding how and why community development and vibrant communities of Jesus followers among the least reached are connected.
   - The Kingdom is 'already and not yet'. It is about *shalom*, a growing fulness and wholeness of life.
   - 'Your kingdom come' is a prayer for today that will be fulfilled in the 'new heavens and new earth'. Because God reigns over all creation and all aspects of human life, we seek to align our lives and ministries with this prayer of Jesus.
   - In Scripture and church history, there is an emphasis on the poor and vulnerable that reflects the character of our just and compassionate God and the nature of his Kingdom.

2. Our understanding of how people enter the Kingdom of God will affect how we do ministry.
   - 'Doing good' is important in most religions. This gives community development workers the freedom to identify themselves as God-fearing and as Jesus followers.
   - Rooted in love, our behaviour and attitudes set the focus on Christ and build trust. As trust is built, questions are asked that provide natural opportunities to share our motivation and faith. Some will go on to engage with the Bible's story and begin a journey toward transformation, finding their true identity in Christ.

3. The gospel impacts the whole person and people's whole contexts.
    - We are not trying to balance proclamation and demonstration as if they are two different things. We want to be a witness through all we are and do: our lives, words, and deeds.
    - An integrated witness leads to a deeper and stronger transformation of lives and communities, including our own. The gospel, when properly understood, changes everything, both individual and community life. We need a theology that helps people understand suffering, poverty, and injustice.
    - Integral mission, including community development, is not a programme or project. It is how we live every aspect of our lives, both who we are in Christ and what we do as we join in with the mission of God.
    - Intentionality is vital. We are always ready to give an answer to the faith and hope within us (1 Pet. 3:15).
    - We are careful to avoid using community development to create a 'platform', but we realise that engagement with a community through development offers access to the least reached from a credible position that truly demonstrates the amazing depth and breadth of God's love, whether people respond to that love or not.

4. Our motivation is to glorify Christ. We long for people to come to faith in him, but our vision does not stop there. We want to see the Kingdom of God impact people and the communities we live in.
    - We rest in God's sovereignty and timing; a lack of visible spiritual fruit is not necessarily a sign of failure.
    - One sign of the Kingdom's presence is that we serve and meet needs as Jesus did because people are needy. Like the

Ten Principles

exiles from Judea in Babylon, we seek the whole city's welfare, not just for our own good but for theirs as well (Jer. 29:7).

5. Spiritual warfare and prayer are an integral part of community development.
   - Acting with and for justice is a form of fasting (Isa. 58), undermining systemic injustice an aspect of spiritual warfare.
   - We may not be able to measure our impact nor explain the impact we do see.
   - As we work for God's Kingdom, we should expect opposition; worship, praise, prayer, and fasting accompany our work.

6. Creation glorifies, praises, and witnesses to God. Caring for creation is an act of worship. Our concern for creation is an act of obedience to God and participation in his work of reconciling all things to himself.
   - Community development approaches that demonstrate good stewardship of the environment help promote the care of creation among the communities we serve.
   - Individually, and as organisations, we live out this concern aware that how we live has an impact both nearby and far away.

7. Community development will only be truly transformational if it brings a vision for vibrant communities of Jesus followers and the renewal of the whole person and community.
   - A truly vibrant community of Jesus followers obeys all that Jesus commanded (Matt. 28:18–20).
   - A truly vibrant community of Jesus followers shows the fruit of the Spirit to one another and to the wider community; they

Undivided Witness

gather together and also serve by engaging, blessing, and seeking the good of their community.
- Individual discipleship and leadership training must include equipping for transformational community engagement.

8. Community development workers are committed to professional excellence.
   - Faith-based entities that are aligned to a biblical understanding of God's mission provide an environment that shapes the motivation of workers and is attractive to the community.
   - Following ethical and professional standards is vital. This will help us avoid things such as creating dependency, trying to 'buy' allegiance, or thinking we have all the answers and have nothing to learn from the community.

9. There is significant overlap between the principles of excellence in community development and working toward the formation of vibrant communities of Jesus followers, including:
   - Commitment to serve the least reached
   - Working collaboratively
   - Adopting locally reproducible approaches
   - Living incarnationally
   - Solidarity with those who suffer
   - Benefiting the whole community and sowing the seeds of the gospel widely
   - Focus on teamwork
   - Focus on groups and the existing community
   - Empowering people and making disciples, not 'converts'
   - Local leadership and local ownership

Further, the community development sector offers familiar and accepted strategies involving a mix of international and local experts who work together and in partnership with local civil society organisations. This increasingly includes partnering with churches and other faith communities.

10. The 'least reached' are so for a reason, both spiritually and often in terms of poverty and development.
- The least reached are often hidden, separated not just from us but also from their own society by hostile environments, disease, gender, and other complex factors.
- When we make the extra effort to find, come alongside, understand, and serve them, we may find ourselves in places where we were not expected, a pleasant surprise that may open hearts and minds to the service and love Christ compels us to offer.

PRINCIPLE 1: UNDERSTANDING THE KINGDOM OF GOD IS FUNDAMENTAL

JONATHAN WILLIAMS

Ten or so years ago I visited a village while working with a well-known international evangelical denomination and mission movement. The village was low caste and in a desperately poor, fundamentalist Hindu state. The organisation ran a self-help group programme in such villages facilitated by members of the church who had basic training in setting up women's self-help groups. They were known as field organisers (FOs). The aim of these groups was to establish a micro-saving and micro-lending system, provide a structure for training in livelihood skills, and promote collective action to address social, economic, spiritual, and environmental issues their community might be facing.

In a particular village, the FO was making good progress with one newly empowered group that had confronted unjust landowners who wanted to sell productive village land to a plantation owner. This would have not only taken needed farmland away from the villagers but would likely create environmental issues with irrigation from scarce groundwater resources, chemical leaching, and soil erosion. The landowners were attempting to divide the villagers socially through an unequitable system of compensation. The self-help group was saving and lending successfully; a number of women had started small businesses or helped their husbands to do so. The FO helped the women to start a micro-saving fund to help manage the relentless run of religious feast days. A deep connection with this group of women was forming.

One day, the women of the group asked the FO if she was married. She replied that she was, and they asked why she was not adorned with the jewellery of a traditional Hindu wife. She explained that, as a follower of Jesus, she was not required to. This sparked significant interest. The women asked more about her faith and whether there was a Holy Book that they might see. On the next visit, she brought her Bible and, as the women were illiterate, read to them. In time, two of the women gave their lives to Jesus.

In the Hindu beliefs of that area, women who had committed to Jesus were no longer considered 'their' people and, although still part of the group, they faced persecution from neighbours. One day, the child of a believer became very sick. The doctors said the child would die without a transfusion. Due to their status of being outside of the Hindu faith, none of their neighbours dared donate blood. The FO was called; she donated and also prayed for healing. The child made a miraculous recovery. The combination of the miraculous healing and the love of the FO compelled many more in the community toward Jesus and today there is a VCJF in that community.

Jesus spoke a lot about 'The Kingdom of God' or 'The Kingdom of Heaven'. In recent years, reference to the Kingdom has become prominent in theological reflection. Kingdom theology is a lens to view not only the life of Jesus but the meta-narrative of human history and the future. In this chapter, I examine the importance of using this lens in shaping our community development work, seeking an end to poverty, and going about our work in a way that will bear the fruit of transformed lives, communities and nations.

As a good student and practitioner of community development, project frameworks are never far from my mind. Love them or hate them, most of us working in community-based projects must deal with them at some point. I have framed some of the issues we will tackle in this light. Understanding the pictures and nature of the Kingdom of God helps me in working among the least reached in the following ways: it expands my expectation of how God works, thus elevating my goals; it expands my understanding of the gospel, which shapes my activities and indicators of success; it gives me a framework to understand unexpected consequences of my work; and it gives me a toolbox for working among the least reached.

THE KINGDOM: CREATION THROUGH JESUS

God's sovereign power as King is seen in creation, the concept of his Kingdom woven throughout the Old Testament history of Israel. As a brief example, Christopher Wright refers to Psalm 33:

> *Not only in Genesis 1 but also in the worship of Israel the link was made between the word of the Lord and the creation of the cosmos.*
>
> *By the word of the Lord were the heavens made,*
> *Their starry host by the breath of his mouth...*
> *For he spoke, and it came to be;*
> *He commanded, and it stood firm. (Ps. 33:6, 9)*
>
> *The same psalm moves from the sovereignty of the word of God in creation to his governing role in history.*
>
> *The Lord foils the plans of the nations;*
> *He thwarts the purposes of the peoples.*

Principle 1

> *But the plans of the Lord stand firm for ever,*
> *The purposes of his heart through all generations. (Ps. 33:10–11)[1]*

The Exodus and subsequent covenant demonstrate God's love and kingship over Israel and, with it, heaven's reclamation of humanity. God is King: 'The Lord will reign forever and ever' is the exultant conclusion of Moses and Miriam, east of the Red Sea (Exo. 15:18). The Davidic monarchy is a picture of God's process of establishing his rule and of what life is like under his rule. The prophets give a Kingdom promise of what is in store for its subjects when the Kingdom is inaugurated in the King's Son.[2]

Jesus fulfils these prophecies, but also makes some potentially confusing statements: The Kingdom will come (Matt. 24), has come (Luke 17:20–21; Matt. 12:28), is coming immediately (Mark 1:15; Matt. 10:23; Luke 21:32), and will be delayed (Matt. 25:1–13; Luke 12:11–27). These varied descriptions give rise to what many describe as the 'now and the not yet' of the Kingdom of God, a concept I will discuss later.

Jesus' life demonstrates to us what subjects of the Kingdom will look like. It tells us what we will say and do—and who we will be. Evangelicalism places a lot of emphasis on the death and resurrection of Jesus, and quite rightly so. But his life is equally important in understanding what he came to die for and consequently how we should live. Rediscovering the person and life of Jesus has been central to the work of many theological thinkers as they seek to understand the relevance of the Kingdom of God.

THE KINGDOM INAUGURATED

'Inaugurated eschatology' is the idea that Jesus 'inaugurates' the Kingdom of God on Earth. However, does not God rule the universe and not just Earth? Pastor and theologian Derek Morphew draws our attention to the references in Daniel, later picked up by Jesus, that talk about 'the present age' and 'the age to come'. He suggests that in Jesus' death and resurrection the power of the 'age to come' breaks into this age. That same power is available to us as the subjects of his Kingdom. God's rule extends to

> *...all reality, yet we do not necessarily experience his rule in our lives. The coming of the kingdom involves God's intervention in the course of human history. His power breaks into the affairs of men, confronting the forces that*

withstand him and imprison people, and interrupting the normal course of society.[3]

But what does this mean in practice?

When I helped the project officer write the proposal for the project in the story at the beginning of the chapter, we did not anticipate the outcome we now can see. Together we saw the Kingdom of God was established:
- over the natural and supernatural principalities of the landowners (the structures that perpetuated poverty)
- over the sickness of the child
- over the teaching and entrapment of Hinduism
- over the unbelief in the hearts of the other members of the group.

How did that experience affect me? Now, when I write a project proposal, I ask the Holy Spirit what he is doing in a situation and adjust my goal accordingly. Bryant Myers claims that any work with the poor that is not guided, empowered, and made effective by the Spirit will not be sustainable and that 'expecting and praying for supernatural interventions of the Spirit must be part of the spirituality of Christian development workers'.[4]

A goal inspired by an understanding of a picture of the Kingdom and a knowledge of the power of the Kingdom gives a blueprint for prayer and a boost in faith. Proclaiming the Kingdom of God helps to usher it in. The Kingdom is marked by healings, deliverance, and other signs and wonders. The disciples practiced these, as have countless Christians throughout the ages, but if we are not expecting them, we are unlikely to be looking or praying for them and so are less likely to see them.

Consider this challenge: When writing your project proposal or praying for the community you serve, remember that the power of the age to come has come already through the Holy Spirit living in you and is available here and now. Allow that to make a difference in what you expect to see and what you witness.

GOSPEL OF THE KINGDOM

At times I have reduced the message of the gospel to something like this: Jesus, the Son of God, came to Earth, died, and rose again so that all who believe in him might go to heaven when they die. Any signs and wonders are purely to convince people that this gospel is true so

Principle 1

that they can go to heaven when they die. Our overriding mission as Christians is to tell as many people as possible about Jesus so that they do not go to hell.

I lived in two paradigms: my work as a community development worker, and my identity as a Christian with a mission to see souls saved. The first came from a compassion that I believe God has put in my heart for the poor. The second was mostly coming from a feeling of obligation to God and fear for the people who did not believe.

What I had essentially done is reduce the message of the gospel. Rereading my opening story, it is difficult to imagine that the Holy Spirit healed those children and enabled change in the welfare of the community members *only* to save them from hell.

Within Kingdom theology, the concept of salvation takes on a different emphasis from this idea of 'going to heaven when we die'. Anglican theologian and bishop N.T. 'Tom' Wright asserts that:

> *Salvation, then, is not 'going to heaven', but 'being raised to life in God's new heaven and new earth'. But as we put it like this we realize that the New Testament is full of hints, indications and downright assertions that this 'salvation' isn't just something to wait for in the long-distant future. We can enjoy it here and now.*[5]

Matt Hyam draws on the significance of Jesus' continual call 'to' eternal life 'from' destructive ways of thought and life. In his study of John 3:16, Hyam asserts that the call of this passage is to 'partake in something beautiful right now—to enter life as it was always meant to be'. According to his study of the original text and context, he would summarise the invitation as: 'God showed us how much he loved the cosmos by sending his only Son. All you need do is trust him and you will be rescued from spiritual death and begin the new life of the Age to come.'[6]

So what is this new life and what is it like? Kingdom theologians and development thinkers speak about the *shalom* or peace of God. This is a term that implies right, healed, restored relationships on multiple levels. Myers asserts that the meta-narrative of the Bible is this:

> *God's goal is to restore us and God's creation to our original identity and purpose, as children reflecting God's image, and to our original vocation as productive stewards, living together in just and peaceful relationships.[7]*
>
> *Furthermore, the goals of transformation that I have suggested…are derived from the biblical story and are the goals for both the community and the development facilitator. Seeking the truth from the biblical story is the beginning of transformation in our lives and relationships. Therefore, engaging the biblical story must be central to the practice of transformational development done by Christians.[8]*

We can see from the case study a number of areas of broken relationships in the village and in the lives of the villagers. We can also begin to see some of these restored and redeemed through the Holy Spirit working, in part, through the FO.

An understanding of the Kingdom sees a world broken and on a path to destruction because of its separation from the King. The inauguration of the Kingdom in Jesus—to whom all of the Old Testament points (Luke 24:27)—sees the start of the reversal of this brokenness that we are called to be a part of until, one day, God will establish a new and perfect Earth that we will be called upon to tend in our resurrected bodies. We can see a picture of this transformed Earth in prophecies such as Isaiah 65:17–25 and Revelation 21–22.

The FO in the story understood and appreciated the vital importance of the people deciding to enter God's Kingdom. Yet she loved them sufficiently to want the power of the Kingdom to change the physical, social, environmental, and political brokenness they found themselves in. For the FO, there was no distinction between a verbal proclamation, physical support, or a miraculous healing; it was all simply an expression of her living out her new creation, bringing signs and symbols of the Kingdom to birth on Earth and in heaven.

This leads us to the question that many ask: *How do we balance the verbal proclamation with the non-verbal?* Jayakumar Christian reminds us that it is not a case of balance: '[P]roclaiming the Kingdom of God is no mere option. It is *the* most appropriate response to the powerlessness of the poor. The Kingdom of God is the only viable alternative that spells true and complete liberation for the powerless poor.'[9]

Elsewhere, J. Christian beautifully and eloquently describes the moment of a verbal explanation of the gospel thus:

Principle 1

Mission is about being obedient and asking God what he is doing. The poor will understand this language and will say: 'Ah, these people are obedient to their God.' And eventually people would come and ask us: 'So what is the name of this God?' And at that time you should be able to tell your story.[10]

And that is what we see the FO doing in my opening story.

Consider another challenge: Are you seeing the bigger picture of the work of proclaiming the Kingdom in your relationships and community development work? Are you allowing love for God and the people to guide your actions, or is fear or obligation determining them?

DEALING WITH THE UNEXPECTED

Despite our best efforts, we do not always see the outcomes we expect in our work and our personal lives. We pray for someone to be healed, we fast, we blow *shofars,* we anoint with oil, we stand on one leg every day for half an hour (because we heard someone did that once), we purge ourselves of sin and even stop kicking the dog, but the person gets worse and sadly dies. And then the devil starts having fun: Was my faith insufficient? Was the sick person's faith insufficient? Who had secret sin in their lives? Maybe this is God's will so that he will be glorified. Maybe my motives were wrong.

The 'now and not yet' nature of the Kingdom helps us process these moments. The Kingdom has come, yes; we do see healings such as the child in the story. The Kingdom has yet to come, which is why there is still sickness and poverty in that village today. Does it mean that we stop praying and become fatalistic? Not at all! But it does help us to get up, dust ourselves off, and keep praying until we see the Kingdom come. Faith, the breaking of spiritual strongholds, and other factors do appear to be ingredients in healing and transformation, but, as we see in the gospel accounts, there were times when Jesus was not able to heal everyone who came to him, yet he was walking in perfect step with the Spirit. We cannot say that the faith or method of one who prays is the only reason transformation does not always come as hoped for.

Understanding that the Kingdom has not come fully in us is humbling and allows me to correct some of the 'God complexes' I have when I approach poverty alleviation. When I fall short of the standards set by Jesus, I need to avoid the temptation to hide my humanity. I remember one relief effort we undertook in the mountains of Central Asia in a community where we had a number of long-term development projects. I made some significant mistakes that caused division in the community and shredded our reputation. However, we apologised and sought forgiveness. This astonished the villagers, who had never contemplated that an international NGO would seek forgiveness from them. That was a significant Kingdom proclamation. We were able to continue work in this village with a new openness and an authentic relationship.

Yet another challenge: Is there a situation that you have been longing to see God's Kingdom come in power to transform? Take it to him. Continue to pray.

TOOLS FOR THE DEVELOPMENT WORKER

An important development in the Gospels is that the enemy of the Kingdom of God assumes a new shape: 'He is no longer identified with particular nations and the gods that rule them, but with all the evil of the world and all opposition to God. The final cosmic battle has begun.'[11] As ambassadors of the age to come, we are prime targets for spiritual attack where the powers of the age to come meet the powers of the present age. As development workers, we are heading into some of the most dispiriting places on Earth—places devoid of hope where the devil has had powerful dominion for years. The enemy promotes poverty and despair, but the Kingdom of God is about freedom and *shalom*.

On the whole, the materially rich and powerful are so because others are poor and weak. Many readers of this book can be counted as the rich and powerful or part of that broken system. As those who work against poverty and injustice, we are a threat to the powerful—though we perhaps were born into that power—and there is likely to be a physical and spiritual backlash. We catch a glimpse of this in my opening story as the new believers are ostracised and as authorities try to block the just distribution of land belonging to the village. Understanding these concepts of spiritual battle and kingdom clashes has been tremendously helpful in looking to the wellbeing of myself and my team.

In all of this comes a warning. God uses us to build his Kingdom, but '[w]e must not put the weight of kingdom building on our shoulders…the sign of the Kingdom is the church, the community of faith, not the development worker or the development agency.'[12]

Principle 1

And, as N.T Wright has written,

> ...God builds God's kingdom. But God has ordered the world in such a way that his own work within that world would take place not least through one of his creatures in particular, namely the human beings who reflect his image...And, following the disaster of rebellion and corruption, he has built into the gospel message the fact that, through the work of Jesus and the power of the Spirit, he equips humans to help in the work of getting the project back on track.[13]

While the authors of the following chapters offer practical applications of these concepts, I draw attention to the following principles growing out of our understanding of the Kingdom of God—how we go about community development in particular with a vision to see vibrant communities of Jesus followers among the least reached.

We need to pay attention to the **importance of communities in the holistic transformation process**. J. Christian states, 'Community is integral to understanding the trinitarian Kingdom of God. When Kingdom power is expressed it always creates community.'[14] The creation of community is not simply a convenient overlap between good development theory and how we believe the church grows. It goes to the very heart of the nature of the Kingdom of God.

Next is the **importance of teams**. An understanding of the Kingdom should shape our teams. J. Christian talks of 'covenant-quality inclusive relationships' of grassroots practitioners that become a 'hermeneutical community that constantly shapes and reshapes its paradigms and models of mission'. This allows the unreached poor to see Christian community in action but also provides the supportive environment needed for the complex and difficult work they are involved in. He continues, 'Training of grassroots practitioners must affirm the role of the Holy Spirit in mission and plan for intentional spiritual formation...the recognition and use of spiritual gifts must be an integral part of mission that seeks to confront powerlessness of the poor.'[15] There needs to be a recognition that any sustainable change we seek will only come about through the agency of the Spirit, not due to the 'cleverness' or 'effectiveness' of our programmes or approaches.[16] These teams also help us withstand the suffering that, in most cases, is an inevitable consequence of proclaiming the Kingdom.

In addition, the emphasis on **skills in reading God's word** should be emphasised. God will speak to us about his Kingdom purposes in our contexts through his word.

J. Christian expresses clearly an important concept as I think of my call to community development: 'A kingdom-based response equips the poor to be agents of transformation and thus initiate movements.'[17] Our job is to **equip the poor and unreached** with 'the right understandings of kingdom power so that they may initiate ripples of transformation in their world.'

Finally, we need to be **totally dependent on God as we seek his Kingdom**. God's Kingdom is not built by our technique, skill, and programs. In line with Jesus' prayer, 'Your Kingdom come; your will be done', he puts passion in our hearts. Recognising that God builds his Kingdom, that God's Spirit reaches the unreached, I pray not that I myself will reach some community but that the community will be reached. As we seek God for his Kingdom plans, our expectation increases as do the audacity of our prayers and our faith at being part of that in-breaking. Prayer on all levels is vital, as we long to see lasting Kingdom impact in our lives and those of the people we serve.

CONCLUDING THOUGHTS AND CHALLENGES

As you launch deeper into an exploration of what community development might look like among the least reached, I encourage you to think about your current calling and work. What is God doing? What has he called you to do?

I get incredibly excited when I grasp the liberating truth that the Kingdom, this unstoppable *shalom* of healing and wholeness, has come and is coming to the communities and lives I know that need it so badly (not least me). I am excited that God wants to use me to help extend and proclaim his Kingdom as his beloved child and subject. Through the power of the Holy Spirit, the fellowship of his church and truth of the Bible, he has given me everything I need to see his Kingdom come among the least reached.

Principle 1

ENDNOTES

---

[1] Christopher J. H. Wright, *The Mission of God: Unlocking the Bible's Grand Narrative* (Downers Grove: IVP Academic, 2006), 85-86.
[2] Derek Morphew, *Breakthrough: Discovering the Kingdom*, 3rd ed. (Cape Town: Vineyard International, 2001), 53.
[3] Morphew, *Breakthrough*, 2001, 9.
[4] Bryant L. Myers, *Walking with the Poor: Principles and Practices of Transformational Development*, Rev. ed. (Maryknoll: Orbis, 2011), 80.
[5] Tom Wright, *Surprised by Hope* (London: SPCK, 2007), 210.
[6] Matt Hyam, *Life before Death: A Study of Judgment and Eternal Life in John's Gospel* (Southampton: Hopeful Ink, 2018), 50, 51.
[7] Myers, *Walking with the Poor*, 2011, 82.
[8] Myers, *Walking with the Poor*, 2011, 330.
[9] Jayakumar Christian, *God of the Empty-Handed: Poverty, Power and the Kingdom of God*, 2nd Kindle (Brunswick East, Australia: Acorn Press, 2011), sec. 4669.
[10] Jayakumar Christian, 'Aid Agencies, Church and Transformation' (CCDC Conference, Germany, June 2016).
[11] Morphew, *Breakthrough*, 2001, 62.
[12] Myers, *Walking with the Poor*, 2011, 77.
[13] Wright, *Surprised by Hope*, 2007, 218.
[14] Christian, *God of the Empty-Handed*, 2011, sec. 4060.
[15] Christian, *God of the Empty-Handed*, 2011, sec. 4765.
[16] Myers, *Walking with the Poor*, 2011, 84.
[17] Christian, *God of the Empty-Handed*, 2011, sec. 4786.

Principle 2: Understanding How People Enter the Kingdom of God Shapes How We Do Ministry

David Greenlee

In 2015 Joy* and an AIDSLink teammate visited an HIV care centre in Southeast Asia. There they met a man who had no hope. Unaware that he was selling his medications rather than taking them as prescribed, the pair encouraged him to take care of himself, explaining how the medications work. 'Your wife and child need you alive,' they lovingly reminded him before praying for him.

During a visit to the centre in 2019, a healthy man approached Joy and asked if he remembered him. Such a transformation had taken place that Joy did not realise that he had crossed paths again with the once-desperate man. 'I am the person you met five years ago at the care centre,' he said. 'You encouraged me to take my medication and prayed for me.' Soon after, he had started taking his antiretroviral therapy drugs rather than selling them, gradually growing stronger. 'You also shared the gospel with me,' he continued, 'and now I am a follower of Jesus.' His wife and children are also part of a local fellowship of believers.

THE GOODNESS OF THE GOOD NEWS

Richard Peace observes that 'how we conceive of conversion determines how we do evangelism'.[1] I expand and mirror his thought to suggest that the way we go about ministry reflects our understanding of the Kingdom of God.

With that in mind, what was good about the good news for you?

For me, not quite seven years old, I was drawn to the promise of eternal life. Howard Jones, one of Billy Graham's associate evangelists, had preached at our Methodist church in a small American town dominated by the seminary where my father was a professor. At Rev. Jones's invitation, I slipped away from my parents and hurried to the front where I knelt and prayed. What dark, six-year-old sins did I confess? I cannot remember. But the next day, having been threatened by some mean ten-year-olds we must have annoyed, I told my friend Bobby, 'Well, it wouldn't matter if they had killed us. I gave my heart to Jesus last night, and I would have gone to heaven.'

For some of us, our coming to faith and how we tend to go about evangelism are focused on the problem of guilt. Especially in societies with Christian roots, most of us know we are guilty of something, but we might not know what to do about it. The goodness of the good news is forgiveness, assurance that the guilt is taken away. John's declaration is a vital promise: 'If we confess our sins, he is faithful and just and will forgive our sins and purify us from all unrighteousness' (1 John 1:9). It goes along with Peter's assurance that Jesus himself 'bore our sins in his body on the cross so that we might die to sins and live for righteousness...' (1 Pet. 2:24).

Others among us might not carry a strong sense of guilt, or at least it is not at the front of our thinking. Instead, like others in our society, engrained into our souls is a sensitivity to issues of honour and shame. We work hard to maintain peace and harmonious relationships (at least outwardly) but we find ourselves separated from those we love, from ourselves, and from God. Like the younger son who squandered his father's generosity, as told in Jesus' famous parable, in honest moments we might recognise that 'I don't deserve to be called your son or daughter' (Luke 15:19). The goodness of the good news for those with this mindset might be that by bearing the shame of the cross (Phil. 2:5–11), Jesus dealt with our shame; honour is restored, and relationships renewed. In Jesus we find that 'the one who believes in him will never be put to shame' (Rom. 9:33b).

Related to the issue of shame and honour is the problem of purity. Defilement was a continual issue for the peoples of the Bible. It was not just diseases like leprosy that caused separation from others but even normal functions of the body and, for women, times of the month. Impurity also caused separation from God: '"Woe to me!" I cried. "I am ruined! For I am a man of unclean lips and I live among a people of unclean lips, and my eyes have seen the King, the Lord Almighty,"' lamented the young prophet (Isa. 6:5). Impurity remains a perpetual problem for masses of humanity today; just think of Hindu rituals of washing in the Ganges River or ablutions carried out before Muslim prayers. The good news is good for those aware of their impurity. Forgiveness is the oft-emphasised part of

Principle 2

the assurance offered in 1 John 1:9; purification from all unrighteousness is equally part of that promise.

And what about those like the cultural Chinese, guided by a background mixture of Confucian thought, Daoism, and Buddhism? I'Ching Thomas tells us that while issues of honour and shame are vitally important to those formed by this view, maintaining honour contributes to fulfilling a more comprehensive need: the desire for human flourishing. This vital concept in Confucian understanding is rooted in good relationships: father–son, elder brother–younger brother, husband–wife, elder–junior, and ruler–subject. Confucian teaching fails, though, to help us find a way to achieve this through our own merit and ability. The goodness of the good news for cultural Chinese and others rooted in Confucian thinking is that, through Jesus, our relationship with God our Father can be mended. Rooted in that, our relationships with others can be restored as well, in turn leading to true flourishing.[2]

TIMING AND DIRECTION

Beyond these differences in what attracted us to Jesus' good news, there are also differences in timing. No one-size-fits-all timeline captures the life stories of those who know Jesus.

For some, there will be a clear point in time when they knew that they had received the gift of eternal life, a climactic change like Paul's on the Damascus Road—as was my own experience as a young boy. For others, like Peter or John in the Gospels, it may be harder to pinpoint a specific time of 'coming to faith'. This was the case for Muhammad, a young man I met in Sri Lanka. Unlike me, he cannot point to a specific point in time when he turned in faith to Jesus. What he does know, with full assurance, is that while once he did not believe, today he does—the result of a process of gradual steps of turning.[3]

Paul Hiebert applied a mathematical concept to missiology to help us understand something of this process/point issue and the related question of boundaries.[4] Centred sets are groups related by a common centre. Some fans of a sports team are true fanatics while others are casual supporters. Whatever else distinguishes their lives, their shared team support gives them a common centre. Bounded sets describe those who have crossed a certain boundary. I am an alumnus of my university; you (probably) are not. The only way for you to join my alumni association is to first earn a degree, not from any university but from my university.

There are certain features of being a member of God's Kingdom that fit into the concept of bounded sets. Legalistic approaches and 'keeping the rules' will not get you in; Paul considered them rubbish (Phil. 3:1–11). When I search the New Testament, though, I find one clear factor, a sort of boundary that distinguishes those who have the promise of eternal life from those who do not: believing in Jesus.

In an extended discussion of New Testament terms associated with conversion, Colin Brown notes that, while often used separately, in the 'repent and turn' phrases of Acts 3:19 and 26:20, the words *metanoeō* and *epistrephō* are used side by side. This, Brown says, 'shows that the two concepts are related. In these cases, *metanoeō* describes rather the turning from evil and *epistrephō* the turning to God.'[5] Turning predicates a change of direction, a new centre much more than barriers of behaviour and membership.

In our opening story, the man living with HIV turned in faith to Jesus Christ fairly soon after his discussion with Joy. His knowledge was limited, but what he saw and heard gave him hope. Soon joined by his wife, their direction centred on Jesus and they grew closer to him, encouraged by the small fellowship they had joined, they said. Distance from Jesus in the sense of detailed biblical and theological knowledge did not separate them from God's saving grace. Moving closer to Jesus as their centre was part of the process of discipleship.

While the notion of centred sets is frequently discussed in missiological writing, there is a related concept Hiebert discussed that we often overlook: the idea of fuzzy sets. When I flip a switch on my office wall, the light turns on; there is no fuzzy 'half-on' state. Years ago, when I spent many years at sea, on clear mornings I could distinctly tell when the sun had risen above the horizon; only a brief moment passed between the top edge of the sun appearing and its brilliant full circle being visible. What happened on foggy or rainy mornings? My observations were less precise. At one point I knew it was night, and eventually that it was day. But, hidden by the clouds, I could not say with precision when the sun crossed the horizon. A long period of twilight marked that uncertainty.

As described in the opening story of our book's Introduction, a community in Central Asia is taking their time as they consider Jesus. They are attracted to him; their knowledge and understanding

Principle 2

of God is growing through the Bible stories they learn and the lives of community development workers they observe. But Jesus, as far as we know, is not yet their centre; to our observation they have not yet repented and turned (Acts 26:20) to him in faith. In their case, knowing who has come to faith is something of a fuzzy set, like the twilight on a foggy morning at sea. Eventually, we trust that the sun will rise; they will clearly and openly follow Jesus. But for now, as the workers continue to serve and shine Jesus' love into hearts, only God's Spirit truly knows if any among them have entered the Kingdom.

ENTERING THE KINGDOM

Whatever the attraction to the gospel or description of the journey to faith, certain biblical expressions describe all who enter the Kingdom of God. Most basically, our ability to enter God's Kingdom is itself an act of God. Doing what for us is impossible (Matt. 19:26), God the Father has

> *...qualified you to share in the inheritance of the saints in the kingdom of light. For he has rescued us from the dominion of darkness and brought us into the kingdom of the Son he loves, in whom we have redemption, the forgiveness of sins. (Col. 1:12b–14)*

Several gospel passages describe not who enters, but who is barred from the Kingdom. Some think that they used the right words or did the right deeds, but in fact they have not done the will of the Father. They will be barred from entering the Kingdom because, Jesus tells us, he never knew them (Matt. 7:21–23). Entry is only possible to those who receive the Kingdom like a little child (Mark 10:15). In stark contrast to godly childlikeness, Mark tells us, those who cling to riches—whatever form they take—will go away sad (Mark 10:17–22). Entering by 'the narrow door' is the only way into the Kingdom. Many who thought they belonged will be cast out while 'people will come from east and west and north and south' together with Abraham, Isaac, Jacob, and all the prophets and 'take their places at the feast in the Kingdom of God.' (Luke 13:22–30).

Who are those, then, qualified by God to enter his Kingdom? Simply it is those who are born again (John 3:3), those who believe in the Son (John 3:16). This kind of belief is not mere assent, nor is it intended to help us merely get a foot in the door—it does so much more! And why, in any case, would we ever be content to have the bare minimum of life in God's Kingdom?

Deeply Rooted Change

> *A young couple entered the lobby of our offices in suburban Atlanta. I was waiting to speak to our receptionist but felt drawn to welcome the visitors who had paused just inside the doors. Initial introductions completed and a cup of coffee shared, they told me their story: job loss, health issues, and eviction from their apartment. As of midday they would be homeless, unable to pay the cheap hotel where they had slept the past few nights; their only option would be to sleep in their car with their young daughter. Only their desperation overcame their shame of asking—begging, they felt—for help. Together with two discerning teammates I drew into the conversation, we pointed the couple to resources to help them find longer-term solutions, as well as covering the immediate challenge of lodging and food.*

Thinking back on this experience, I still wonder about the approach of one of my friends. He had deep compassion for the couple and responded generously from his own resources. But, having quickly established the couple's immediate need, before offering practical help he directly asked each of them, 'If you die tonight, do you know where you are going? Do you trust in Jesus Christ and are you Bible-believing Christians?' Both nodded agreement. I think they were sincere. But how were we to know for sure? His question was vitally and eternally important, but was it the right question? Or, better put, was the timing of the question right?

I think back to an experience during my years living in Zurich. A Muslim refugee recently arrived from West Africa began visiting our church. Welcomed by many, he received gifts that helped him make the adjustment to a cold winter. After several weeks, I was told, he had trusted in Jesus and intended to be baptised. And then he disappeared. Later, I found out, he had settled into the basic comforts of life as an asylum-seeker granted refugee status, but he did not respond to my calls and avoided contact with the church.

Had he milked the system, putting on a spiritual façade to take advantage of generosity? Perhaps, but I prefer a more charitable explanation. Like many refugees in Switzerland, the basics of life were provided by the government. The young man, though, felt lost in this new country, confused, lonely, and often cold. His new acquaintances, from warm hearts, had given him gifts he needed. When some spoke to him of Jesus, how could he do anything but go along? They held the money, the power, the advantage; saying 'no' to them would have brought them dishonour. The refugee could take the pressure for only a few weeks. Eventually, though, the dissonance in his heart grew to the breaking point. His only remedy was to avoid us entirely.

While the African man's home society is certainly a 'least-reached' setting, the locations of these two specific stories were not. I tell them, though, because they are part of my story and because they point to issues important to the focus of this book: issues of ethics and power.

As we point people to Jesus in the 'community development among the least reached' space, will they more likely and more enduringly turn to him from a position of powerless dependency or from strength? Dealing with 'transformational mission' and community development, David Lim addresses this issue.

> *Whether the person or the community turns to Christ or not, we hope that each individual in the populace will have been empowered to become mature and responsible (not dependent) citizens who can make dignified and wise decisions for their individual and communal life (including to be for or against Christ). They would be active participants (not passive or marginalized spectators) in tackling issues that affect their lives and destinies in the light of God's Word.*[6]

Affirming Lim, I consider the story of the crowds fed by Jesus but who could not stomach his words; even some of his disciples turned away (John 6:66). We allow people freedom to accept or reject the good news as we empower them, come alongside them, and act as catalysts to help them address their individual and community needs to the extent that they are confident enough to reject Jesus—or turn to him.

ENGAGED FOR THE LONG TERM
In 2010 my wife and I visited a development project near Banda Aceh, Indonesia. We were amused by a cluster of young boys playfully posing and calling out, 'Foto NGO, Foto NGO-man.' Although most foreign workers and their money were long gone, these children had

grown up accustomed to 'NGO man' as an entertaining and normal feature of life.

As was the case in Banda Aceh following the 2004 tsunami, people are not surprised to see foreign workers in their communities. Niamey (Niger) and Nouakchatt (Mauritania) come to mind, cities I visited several years ago. Capitals of two of the most impoverished nations, they were havens for NGOs and UN agencies. For a time, I could have imagined for myself (at least as a younger, single man), why not live here? There were challenges but the pay was good and, so long as you stayed close to the city, tethered to the safety of your compound, life (for a time) was not too bad. It was no surprise for the local community that such foreigners would come to their country.

I am reminded, though, of a community of Jesus followers, not comfortably nestled into the NGO district of town but living side-by-side with the poorest of the poor on the edge of one of these cities. Over time their neighbours grew accustomed to the outsiders' presence and appreciated their help. Yet was it not something of an ongoing puzzle, seen through local eyes? Why would they so disadvantage themselves to become part of us?

Friends of mine have spent forty years serving peoples of South and Central Asia. Shortly after the Central Asian republics became independent nations, he founded and for fifteen years led an NGO there. Writing about that time, he told me that on two occasions an American ambassador came to his office unsolicited to visit and talk. Both said similar things. It was not the multi-million-dollar aid projects that were making a difference, but

> ...you are the ones who are actually making the difference in these countries for the long term. Because if there are no millions, it does not matter for you. You will stay. You will find creative ways to get things done and squeeze the most out of limited resources and you will persevere because you know it will take ten to fifteen years to see the changes needed, and you will stay until the changes start to happen.
>
> So do not change who you are. Stay true to who you are and do not go after the millions and do not become like these other organisations.

In his study of a major faith-based organisation involved in development, Bob Mitchell came to similar conclusions.

Principle 2

> Long-term commitment is seen as one of the distinctive advantages of faith-based development organizations...Personnel operating from a faith commitment may be more willing to submit themselves to the privations of living with impoverished communities on a long-term basis than those operating out of 'career' rather than 'vocation'...Where values include incarnational living, longer-term engagement is possible.[7]

THE COST OF ENGAGEMENT

In the years up to 2004, Pastor Selvaraj witnessed among the Hindu and Muslim communities along Sri Lanka's eastern coast. It was not without cost. At one point someone fired a gun into the church building where a small group were gathered; his son turned his head at just the right time, losing an earlobe to the bullet but not losing his life. Not far away, in an area dominated by the Tamil Tigers, the pastor was beaten badly. Another time, a grenade was tossed at him as he rode past on his motorbike; it bounced off, failing to explode.

Following the devastation of the 2004 tsunami, Selvaraj longed to help even these who had treated him so badly. He became connected with Gabby Markus and the relief efforts of the National Evangelical Alliance of Sri Lanka. To the great surprise of those who had more than once tried to kill him, Selvaraj rode at the front of the trucks carrying desperately needed supplies. In fact, at first they found it difficult to know how to respond. His loving engagement did not stop with a single visit but continued long past the relief stage into the development and rebuilding efforts, eventually helping those who had lost everything to become settled in their newly built homes.

Once a hated and hunted man, Pastor Selvaraj is now welcomed and accepted—even if other Christians from the outside are not. By no means did all in these communities become followers of Jesus, but several have, and three churches formed.

Pastor Selvaraj doubtless did and still does believe that entering the Kingdom of God is through belief in Jesus Christ. He has changed though, I am confident, in his understanding of how people might be drawn into the Kingdom, and how the loving expression of community development can help overcome hatred, establish trust, and eventually be part of the story of some who have entered in.

ENDNOTES

[1] Richard Peace, *Conversion in the New Testament: Paul and the Twelve* (Grand Rapids: Eerdmans, 1999), 286.

[2] I'Ching Thomas, *Jesus: The Path to Human Flourishing: The Gospel for the Cultural Chinese* (Singapore: Graceworks, 2018), 50–52, 114–15.

[3] David Greenlee, *One Cross, One Way, Many Journeys: Thinking Again about Conversion* (Tyrone, GA: Authentic, 2007), 3.

[4] Paul G. Hiebert, *Anthropological Reflections on Missiological Issues* (Grand Rapids: Baker, 1994), 107–36.

[5] Colin Brown (ed), *The New International Dictionary of New Testament Theology*, vol. 1 (Grand Rapids: Zondervan, 1986), 359.

[6] David S. Lim, 'From Asia: Education for Economic Transformation', *William Carey International Development Journal* Education Issue (5 October 2017), http://www.wciujournal.org/index.php/journal/article/2.-education-for-economic-transformation.

[7] Bob Mitchell, *Faith-Based Development: How Christian Organizations Can Make a Difference* (Maryknoll: Orbis, 2017), 62.

Principle 3: The Gospel Impacts the Whole Person and People's Whole Contexts

Rizalina (Sally) Ababa

'For I was hungry and you gave me something to eat, I was thirsty and you gave me something to drink, I was a stranger and you invited me in, I needed clothes and you clothed me, I was sick and you looked after me, I was in prison and you came to visit me.' (Matt. 25:35–36)

> Since 2001, I have been involved in a work among street children in Cebu, Philippines. One of our projects involved an Alternative Learning System centre, an official, practical option for those who do not fit well in the formal Filipino educational structure. One Friday morning at 10am, five teenagers broke into our Bible study with several ALS learners. These teens attended our Tuesday feeding programme and occasionally joined our classes, but on that day, they did not come for Bible study; they were restless, red-eyed, giggling for no specific reason and annoying the rest of the group.
>
> The staff carried on with the Bible Study, while I took care of the newcomers. Offering food and drinks to calm them down, I eventually was able to engage with them. Just around the corner, they had mugged a passer-by and had been chased by a policeman. Running away, they realised that their best escape was through our centre, which was accessible only through the back street. I could surrender these teens to the police or get to know them better. I chose the latter.

Why the Divide?

Some years ago, I helped a friend establish a foundation to aid scavengers and street children in one city in Mindanao, southern Philippines. As their projects began to thrive, my friend started on a path of believing in and following Jesus. Over time, though, he became discouraged by the attitudes he encountered. 'When I think of Jesus Christ and reflect on his teaching, what he did and how he lived his life, he is the closest thing I can picture of God and anything spiritual,' he told me. 'However, I dislike church leaders and pastors; they are not in touch with realities. I am giving up on Christianity; I cannot be a Christian.'

A few years earlier Bob Moffitt was leading a large ministry in America focused on helping churches demonstrate Christ's love and compassion. Writing from far away but with similar sentiments, he lamented, 'I loved the Lord, but I was angry—very angry—with the church.'[1]

It is one thing for those who do not follow Jesus to have such a view. But why should this be the case among devoted disciples of Christ, especially those who, in obedience to Christ, have given their lives for the transformation of the marginalised and outcasts in society?

Why is it that a number of well-meaning Christians labour tirelessly in proclaiming the gospel (specifically, receiving forgiveness for sin) but remain uninvolved in worsening societal issues—as if the rising HIV/AIDS epidemic, crime rates, poverty, man-made calamities, dysfunctional families, human trafficking, climate change, rampant corruption, and forced labour are 'worldly concerns' left for others and not for the church to meddle with? If the church does respond with acts of compassion, for them it is merely a platform to share the gospel. Yet are not followers of Christ to be witnesses of his redemptive grace for the whole of creation and humanity in all of life's dimensions?

For many decades, this great divide between proclamation and demonstration of the gospel produced endless discourse and research among Bible scholars, church leaders, practitioners of community development, missionaries, and even 'people of the pews' all seeking a balance (or priority) in evangelism and social action. Worldviews and approaches to God's mission were characterised by separating spiritual and secular, godly and worldly, eternal and temporal. But should we try to determine which one is more important instead of how they complement one another, thus embracing the whole gospel by the whole church to the whole world for the whole person as our integral mission? Paul stated, 'God was reconciling the world to himself in Christ, not counting people's sins against them. And he has committed to us the message of reconciliation' (2 Cor. 5:19): Jesus Christ is Lord of the whole of life and creation, and we, his redeemed, are his witnesses.

LEARNING HOW TO NOT NEGLECT THE OTHER
How many of us are active in church life, Bible study, tithing, literature distribution, and our spiritual disciplines but remain oblivious to the people and world around us? We fail to notice children being abused

Principle 3

at home, neglected people with disabilities, underpaid workers, trafficked young girls and boys, exploited farmers, disadvantaged indigenous people, and marginalised people of different races, classes, political persuasions, and religious belief. As Christ chided the hypocritical Pharisees and scribes (Matt. 23:23, Luke 11:42), we too should practice the outer life of justice, mercy, and faithfulness without neglecting our inner life.

Building on the 2001 visit of Operation Mobilisation's ship, *Doulos*, we launched a ministry among street children in Cebu City, conducting weekly Bible classes with them in a park. Soon after we learned of multiple tragedies: a child raped by a neighbour, a boy killed by the stray bullets of a drunk policeman, three kids imprisoned for stealing food, separated parents leaving six children on their own, children dropping out of school one by one, and a whole community displaced due to road expansion. Although unprepared, we decided to be part of the community's journey to fulness in Christ. Slowly, we learned to collaborate with the government, other professionals in the field, and willing churches that provided resources and training.

Nearly two decades later, what was once a Bible class with a handful of street children has become a network helping communities find solutions to their needs. Several churches were planted in the slums of Cebu and on nearby mountains and islands. That simple beginning has grown with the communities to spawn various ministries that engaged different churches, government units, communities, organisations, and individuals with stories of transformation of their own. In the process, we have also changed, growing deeper in our relationship with people in the communities we serve—and with our Lord, who grants us love and grace to serve them faithfully.

SO, WHAT IS INTEGRAL MISSION?

In the final decades of the 20th Century, Ecuadorian theologian C. René Padilla and the Latin American Theological Fraternity helped popularise the term 'integral mission'. According to the Micah Declaration, which draws strongly on Padilla's influence,

> *integral mission or holistic transformation is the church speaking of and living out its faith in Jesus Christ in an undivided way in every aspect of life. It is not simply that evangelism and social involvement are to be done*

alongside each other. Rather in integral mission our proclamation has social consequences as we call people to love and repentance in all areas of life. And our social involvement has evangelistic consequences as we bear witness to the transforming grace of Jesus Christ.

If we ignore the world, we betray the word of God, which sends us out to serve the world. If we ignore the Word of God, we have nothing to bring to the world. Justice and justification by faith, worship and political action, the spiritual and the material, personal change and structural change belong together. As in the life of Jesus, being, doing and saying are at the heart of our integral task.[2]

Looking back on how the concept has been adopted, Padilla reflected:

Although it has recently become fashionable to use the term integral mission, the approach to mission that it expresses is not new. The practice of integral mission goes back to Jesus himself and to the first century Christian church. Furthermore, a growing number of churches are putting this style of mission into practice without necessarily using this expression to refer to what they are doing: integral mission is not part of their vocabulary. It is clear that the practice of integral mission is much more important than the use of this new expression to refer to it...Integral mission, a biblical theological framework, is gradually becoming a part of the vocabulary of those who are pressing for a more holistic approach to the Christian mission, even outside Spanish-speaking evangelical circles.[3]

IF THE CHURCH IS NOT INTEGRAL, WHO WILL BE?

What is the significance of integral mission for the role of the church in community development?

Filipino and other Asian community development practitioners and theologians gathered in Manila in February 2008, the fourth gathering of the Asian Theological Seminary Theological Forum, to explore the strategic role of the church in community transformational development. In a book comprising consultation presentations, Charles Ringma laid out the biblical and theological foundations of the church in serving the poor. He then elaborately presented the long history of the church's involvement in community development from the pre-Constantinian period through the Middle Ages and Reformation era and up to the present. Concepts, methodologies, and perceptions of church involvement

Principle 3

took shape corresponding to the circumstances surrounding these various eras. In this modern era, he said,

The map of world Christianity has radically changed. In the post-Reformation world, Christianity was largely Western. Today, seventy percent of Christians are in the Majority World. And since many of these countries struggle with issues of poverty and many Christians are actually poor, the issue of poverty has come to rest (and agitate) within the bosom of the Church itself. The Church is thus not only concerned about the poor, but the Church itself is the Church of the poor. This calls the Church to a new sense of self-identity, theology and praxis.[4]

Gadiel Isidro, a Filipino systematic theologian, based on his survey of the use of the word 'church' in Greek, Hebrew and a study of Matthew 16:18, advances this definition:

That the true church is a group of people summoned by God through the call of the Gospel...of Jesus Christ...They include both men and women, children and adults, rich and poor, ignorant and educated. They come from every tribe, tongue, people and nation. Thus, this body is called the universal church because it transcends geographical, cultural, educational, sexual and economic boundaries. On the other hand, this community, this assembly can also be identified as a local church because it gathers regularly in a certain locality to worship and receive instructions in the Word of God. This local church is a microcosm of the universal church but is not its perfect replica.[5]

The church is a group of people from different backgrounds united in common faith in Jesus Christ. It is mandated to be the 'light of the world and the salt of the earth' rooted in Christ's mission: to seek that which is lost and preach the good news among the poor, the hurting, the weak, and the oppressed (Luke 4:18-19, 19:10; Matt. 5:17; John 5:37, 39). Since Jesus preached the good news of the Kingdom in both word and deeds, should the church not do the same? Furthermore, the presence of the church in poverty-stricken areas necessitates its involvement in holistic transformational development beyond what its secular counterparts offer. If the church fails to carry out this mandate, who else would?

THIS IS INTEGRAL MISSION

Our work in the Philippines expanded to include tribal communities in Palawan. For many years, the Batak tribe remained resistant to

Christianity resulting from harm caused by early missionaries—until a trained Filipino couple arrived in their community, not as missionaries but as learners. They came with a sincere desire to know more about the tribe and to share any knowledge that would be valuable to the community. For two years, they did no preaching, Bible studies, or evangelism, nor did they present anything about Christianity. As a result, they won the hearts of the whole community, particularly the chieftain.

They introduced herbal medicine that greatly reduced infant mortality, made progress toward eradicating malaria locally, helped the first Batak tribal youth to complete college, planted a church in the community and impacted many other communities associated with this tribal group. Our team offered to build a water system for them, saving the community from water-borne epidemics. When the idea to host an event in Palawan was proposed a few months later, the whole community welcomed the OM team and even sent their people for ministry exposure and training.

The chieftain and the missionary couple are now eager to forge a partnership, allowing us to train their young people in creative ministries and community development. They hope to reach many other tribal communities in Palawan that have yet to hear of God's love. The chieftain, later asked to represent the whole tribal group in the province, is now an elder of the church; the missionary couple has become his advisers, as he represents the tribe to the government.

When other mission agencies arrived with unfulfilled promises and an imbalanced sense of mission, the Batak tribe did not withdraw from Christianity; rather, they have learned to own their journey towards independence by becoming God's witnesses among their own people. This church has since planted three others and is working together with other tribal workers to plant more than fifteen churches on the island.

WHOLE HUMANS

In liberation theology, the concept of humans being made in the image of God is primarily social and economic, not addressing the spiritual depravity of man caused by sin, the source of all wrongdoing[6] and the fundamental cause of poverty, which is spiritual.[7] Eschewing spirituality as fundamental is tantamount to departure from basic

Principle 3

Christian faith. Jesus declared, 'Man does not live on bread alone, but on every word that comes from the mouth of God' (Matt. 4:4). Christ recognised the physical needs of humans, but no one deprived of life's basic needs (food, shelter, and clothing) could be emancipated by merely obtaining these, as attested to by various organisations' numerous reviews.[8] In some cases, years of development efforts created dependency on outside help, making further material assistance pointless in alleviating the root causes of poverty.

Predating the influence of liberation theology itself, this emphasis on social needs greatly affected the evangelical response to the social needs of the community. Steve Corbett and Brian Fikkert note that, in the United States, 'This shift away from the poor was so dramatic that church historians refer to the 1900–1930 era as the 'Great Reversal' in the evangelical church's approach to social problems.' This turning away from efforts toward poverty alleviation 'was fundamentally due to shifts in theology and not—as many have asserted—to government programs that drove the church away from ministry to the poor. While the rise of government programs may have exacerbated the church's retreat, they were not the primary cause.'[9]

This 'Great Reversal' of evangelical churches in the West also spread to evangelical churches around the globe. With the worsening moral and economic state of the world, churches have slowly realised that the mission of the church encompasses the whole of humanity—that Christ's offer of salvation is holistic in responding to the total needs of people and communities. Some groups overemphasise the socio-economic and political condition of humanity to the neglect of people's spiritual needs, while for others spiritual needs are paramount with no regard for socio-economic needs or the political and cultural context of the people at stake.

Whether rooted in the history of 'social action' debates among (mainly Western) Christians of the early 1900s or the Latin America-rooted emphasis on liberation theology from the middle of that century, one 'unintegral' approach lays too much emphasis on physical needs and social structures. As spiritual beings, humans need more than today's food—we need the God-given hope of eternal life. Further, as explored by Holly Steward in Chapter 5, spiritual forces are at play in the world that must be addressed for true transformation to occur in individual lives and communities.

Any attempt to disintegrate the wholeness of humans only impedes the desired impact.

But there is an opposite danger, a second 'unintegral' approach. In his plenary address to the 2019 Evangelical Missiological Society's Canada regional meeting, Rupen Das addressed this concern:

> *Those western Christian agencies that try to respond usually bring an evangelist who preaches a standardized Gospel message focusing on sin, forgiveness and repentance. Recent research on conversion among the poor in the global south [sic] shows what attracts the majority of the poor is a God who is responsive, understands their suffering, and is with them—a God who identifies himself as Immanuel. It was only later that they began to understand the issues of sin and forgiveness. Their faith is based on a lived reality of the living God revealed in Jesus Christ rather than on an intellectually robust Christianity based on a platonic separation of the spiritual from the physical. For the non-westerner spiritual experience is followed by understanding, while for the westerner it is the reverse. So rather than presenting a God who is compassionate in the midst of their suffering, the evangelists start with human failure and a God who is judge, yet willing to forgive, a message that does not necessarily resonate with those who are suffering. The focus is on God who is Savior rather than Immanuel.*[10]

However, through the years I have seen how this 'unintegral approach' is deeply influencing the global church. It is no longer simply about differing worldviews from different geographical settings. Instead, as my colleagues note in referring to Das's comments,

> *We agree with Das concerning the nature of God, our message among the poor, and their likely response. We would suggest, though, that this is not a problem of the West alone. Numerous western agencies thoughtfully, integrally communicate the love of God in the ways here affirmed by Das. Meanwhile, well-meaning Global South evangelists have also caused harm by the kind of thoughtless proclamation Das ascribes to western agencies, approaches that failed to meet the standards of truly integral mission, not truly reflecting God's love and grace.*[11]

NOT JUST A PROJECT

A holistic development approach from a Christian perspective takes into consideration the integral needs of humans made in the image of God with spirit, soul, and body. Humans' complex needs cannot be adequately addressed by meeting one need while neglecting others.

Principle 3

The church's mission is no longer and has never been confined within the four walls of the church building, its denominational policies, and proselytising. As Melba Maggay wrote,

> *Timelessness and universality are in the nature of faith traditions. The Christian gospel is always new wine with something to say to all times and all cultures. Unfortunately, its wineskins—those structures and established norms by which we live and proclaim it—are always getting old...Usual ways of doing evangelism and mission, mostly framed within western historical contexts, no longer work in a multicultural world.[12]*

David Lim, a strong advocate of the house church movement in Asia and founder of several mission groups in the Philippines, asserts that 'Mission is Possible' to reach the rest of the world with the gospel through a radical paradigm shift away from traditional missiological approaches to a more integral or 'incarnational' approach because

> *...the visible result of incarnational mission is not in religious buildings (cathedrals or temples) for performing religious ceremonies (liturgies) led by religious leaders (pastors or priests), which often separate believers from their community and divide themselves into different denominations. Instead it is seen in transformed communities that experience peace, justice and righteousness emanating from their love for Jesus and for one another that emerges from their intimate fellowship, which discuss and apply God's word facilitated by any believer who has been discipled by an earlier believer in a micro/simple/house church (in any building); existing church buildings may be turned into multi-purpose ministry centers, like the synagogues in New Testament times.[13]*

Integral mission is not merely another approach to mission; it is a lifelong intentional commitment of our whole being, words, and acts. As we bear witness to the redeeming power of the gospel, it changes both us and the people we serve. May we welcome integral mission with an openness to learn and discover, seeing his will be done, his Kingdom come here on earth, as it is in heaven (Matt. 6:10).

THE JOYS AND SORROWS OF INTEGRAL MISSION

Ten years later, what happened to the five teenagers from my opening story? One graduated with a bachelor's degree in mechanical engineering through our scholarship programme and is now applying for sea-faring internship; he hopes to join Operation Mobilisation's ship, *Logos Hope*. A second lad is now in high school; the third was imprisoned for two years and now sells bottled water on the street. The fourth died in circumstances related to illegal drug raids, and the fifth is working for a politician.

My friend, despite his continued dislike of the church, has worked closely with a Christian training institution, allowing his staff and himself to be trained in Community Transformational Development using integral mission as a framework. Bob Moffitt launched Harvest Foundation and became co-founder of Disciple Nations Alliance, continuing to work around the world 'training local church leaders and congregations about the biblical imperative to live out their faith in word and deed—starting with local resources.'[14]

ENDNOTES

[1] Bob Moffitt, *If Jesus Were Mayor: How Your Local Church Can Transform Your Community* (Oxford: Monarch, 2006), 6.

[2] Micah Network, 'Declaration on Integral Mission' (27 September 2001), https://www.micahnetwork.org/sites/default/files/doc/page/mn_integral_mission_declaration_en.pdf.

[3] C. René Padilla, 'What Is Integral Mission?' (Fox River Grove, IL: Del Camino Network for Integral Mission in Latin America), accessed 13 February 2020, http://www.dmr.org/images/pdf%20dokumenter/C._Ren%C3%A9_Padilla_-_What_is_integral_mission.pdf.

[4] Charles Ringma, 'Liberation Theologians Speak to Evangelicals: A Theology and Praxis of Serving the Poor', in Lee Wanak (ed), *The Church and Poverty in Asia*, ATS Theological Forum (Mandaluyong City, Philippines: OMF Literature, 2008), 27.
Available online at http://docshare.tips/church-and-poverty-in-asia_59346f75ee3435c20663769c.html.

5 Gadiel T. Isidro, *Systematic Theology: Doctrine of Man and the Church* (Cebu City, Philippines: Cabajar Publishing, 2005), 9.
6 Lee Wanak (ed), 'Liberation Theologian: A Position Paper', in *The Church and Poverty in Asia*, ATS Theological Forum (Mandaluyong City, Philippines: OMF Literature, 2008), 247.
7 Bryant L. Myers, *Walking with the Poor: Principles and Practices of Transformational Development*, Rev. ed. (Maryknoll: Orbis, 2011), 144.
8 Turid Sato and William E. Smith, 'The New Development Paradigm: Organizing for Implementation', in Jo Marie Griesgraber and Bernhard G. Gunter (eds), *Development: New Paradigms and Principles for the Twenty-First Century, vol. 2, Rethinking Bretton Woods* (London: Pluto Press, 1996), 89, https://pdfs.semanticscholar.org/173e/dafbde78d0beccb13310bbd3c7f0a9e8a8a4.pdf.
9 Steve Corbett and Brian Fikkert, *When Helping Hurts: How to Alleviate Poverty without Hurting the Poor—and Yourself*, New ed. (Chicago: Moody, 2012), 44.
10 Rupen Das, 'The Mission of God and the Role of Humanitarian Agencies in Responding to the Global Crisis' in Narry F. Santos and Mark Naylor (eds), *Mission Amid Global Crises: Academy, Agency, and Assembly, Perspectives from Canada* (Carol Stream, IL: Tyndale, 2020).
11 David Greenlee et al., 'Exploring the Intersection of Community Development, the Least Reached, and Emerging, Vibrant Churches', *Transformation* 37.2 (April 2020), 105-118, https://doi.org/10.1177/0265378819886223.
12 Melba Padilla Maggay, 'Integral Mission: What's It All About?', in Integral Mission Training Module (Pasig City, Philippines: Institute for Studies in Asian Church and Culture, 2008), 6, https://www.micahnetwork.org/sites/default/files/doc/library/integralmissiontrainingmodule_imi-tng-001.pdf.
13 David S. Lim, 'Towards Closure: Imperial or Incarnational Missions?', *Asian Missions Advance* 33 (October 2011), 20. Available at http://ewcenter.org/wp-content/uploads/2014/08/ama_33.pdf.
14 Moffitt, *If Jesus Were Mayor*, 2006, 7.

Principle 4:
A Broad Vision of Glorifying Christ

Gabriel (Gabby) Markus

Whether responding to a recent crisis or engaging a setting marked by ongoing poverty, what is our motivation for engaging in relief and development efforts? Sharing a desire to serve God, people respond in different ways.

I have coordinated relief and community development efforts in Sri Lanka following the 2004 tsunami and in Greece in response to the refugee crisis that began in 2015. Among those involved I have known some who seemed to focus on immediate needs—food, water, shelter—while others offered some level of assistance but placed a priority on evangelism. At times I have sensed that those who gave priority to evangelism thought that those providing humanitarian assistance were not doing spiritual work, since they were 'only' caring for physical needs of the people. And I have also known humanitarian workers who seemed to think that the other group *just didn't care.*

Why should we divide and give priority to one emphasis or the other? Whatever activities we do, whether proclamation or demonstration of the love of God, it is for the glory of God. We see the importance of both; the difference in focus may be a matter of timing, but we are concerned about both this life and the life to come (1 Tim. 4:8).

We long for people to come to faith in Jesus Christ and for vibrant communities of Jesus followers to be formed. We do not, however, perceive a lack of evident spiritual response as failure; rather, we are called to serve faithfully and trust God for the fruit. We know that an abundant harvest is not always gathered by the first generation of workers (John 4:35–38). This is, in part, a matter of timing.

But what of those settings where, even over a long period, there is no response? We know that not all will turn to faith in Christ, despite our longings. Conditions in Babylon may well have improved as the Jewish exiles sought its welfare (Jer. 29:7) but we are not aware of a great turning to the God of Israel. Jesus healed scores of people because they needed healing; the condition of their lives improved yet not many understood the sign and received him as their Messiah. In our own work, we must never let go of our longing for people to turn to Jesus. Nevertheless, we follow Jesus' example by helping those in need even if they do not respond in faith.

The timing of people coming to faith in Jesus is beyond our control; God is responsible for that. However, it is within our sphere of influence to love and care for the needy and also proclaim the message of salvation. People can experience the presence of the Kingdom of God as we, its people, respond to the needs around us.

RESPONDING TO THE REFUGEE CRISIS IN GREECE

During the 2015–2016 refugee crisis in Greece, our Operation Mobilisation (OM) team was among the first respondents. When the refugees arrived in Athens from the islands, some would spend at least a day in the city, but most would head straight to the border and cross over, bound for other Western European countries. After a few months, the border was closed, and many refugees remained in Athens.

One rainy night, many of them living around Victoria Square went to the nearby Metro station to stay dry. In this crisis they were temporarily moved to the Faliro Tae Kwon Do Stadium built for the 2004 Olympic Games. The next morning, OM workers and several pastors went to the site and helped to arrange food and other items for the refugees. A few weeks later, the refugees were relocated to Galatsi and to the empty buildings of the old airport south of Athens.

Along with the evangelical churches, our team continued to provide relief assistance to refugees in both camps. Some of our workers would be the first to arrive in the morning and the last to leave at night.

One day, someone flew to Greece with an intention to 'evangelise' the refugees but with limited understanding of the situation (or desire to inquire). She had only a short time to 'serve God' before returning to her normal life. After a few days of distributing Bibles and other Christian literature in the camp, she returned to her country satisfied that her mission was completed.

Principle 4

A few days later, the evangelical churches received a letter from the government informing them that they were no longer allowed to work in any refugee camp. Despite being the first respondents to help, they were henceforth banned. Additionally, several refugees who were seen with the Bibles and Christian literature were stabbed and hospitalised. In fear for their safety, they were moved out of the camp and accommodated at a Filipino church with which we had been closely working.

What happened to the refugees? Since 2015, the evangelical churches and the OM team have continued to develop relationships among the refugees, opening their doors to implement projects and helping them find ways to meet their physical needs. Some became followers of Christ, were baptised, and continue to follow Jesus. Some trusted in Christ but later walked away and many, of course, never made a commitment to follow Christ. We later realised that some were baptised just to get a certificate to help with their asylum application.

Recently I asked several of those who have continued following Christ why they made that decision. Most of them indicated one of three reasons:

- 'We were taught that you are the infidels, and we are not to associate with you. We were taught to hate you or even worse. But when we came to Greece, you were among the first to provide for our needs—you love us.'
- 'We did not have the freedom to read the Bible. We were taught that it was manipulated and corrupted. But here, we can read it ourselves, and in doing so, we discovered the truth.'
- Some claimed that they were disaffected with Islam. 'If Islam is a peaceful religion, then why are we killing each other?' they had wondered.

People turned to Christ because of the way Christians reflected the love of God to them not only with words but also with actions. Some turned to Christ for a different motive; yet others turned to Christ out of conviction that Jesus is Lord.

PRIORITY OR INTEGRAL?

Since the famous 1910 World Missionary Conference in Edinburgh, Scotland, the understanding of mission held by churches around the world has developed but also diverged. While Edinburgh's watchword was 'the evangelisation of the world in this generation', the World Council of Churches' 1972 Bangkok assembly considered 'salvation today' to equally include spiritual and socio-political aspects.[1]

In the 'Wheaton Declaration' of 1966, some 1000 delegates from 71 countries expressed their understanding of mission in other ways. The 'evangelistic mandate' was deemed crucial, preaching the gospel to every tribe, tongue, and nation considered the supreme task of the church. Having said that, the Declaration later confesses, 'We are guilty of an unscriptural isolation from the world that too often keeps us from honestly facing and coping with its concerns.'[2] Evangelism was prioritised for soteriological reasons; demonstration of God's concern for social justice and human welfare, the declaration states, should be included whenever possible.

The landmark Lausanne Covenant of 1974 affirmed in its section 'Christian Social Responsibility' that 'evangelism and socio-political involvement are both part of our Christian duty.' Under 'The Church and Evangelism', the previous words were tempered: 'In the Church's mission of sacrificial service, evangelism is primary.'[3]

Documenting further study of this theme by evangelicals, the 1982 'Grand Rapids Report' highlighted three aspects of the relationship: social action as the consequence of, bridge to, and partner with evangelism. Exploring this final theme, the writers note that evangelism and social responsibility

> ... are like the two blades of a pair of scissors or the two wings of a bird. This partnership is clearly seen in the public ministry of Jesus, who not only preached the gospel but fed the hungry and healed the sick. In his ministry, kerygma (proclamation) and diakonia (service) went hand in hand. His words explained his works, and his works dramatized his words. Both were expressions of his compassion for people, and both should be of ours. Both also issue from the lordship of Jesus, for he sends us out into the world both to preach and to serve.[4]

Some, though, wondered about this priority. As Sally Ababa notes in the previous chapter, Ecuadorian theologian C. René Padilla and the Latin American Theological Fraternity helped popularise the term 'integral mission.' Building on Padilla's work, the Micah

Principle 4

Network affirms that this concept is rooted in Scripture. It has its origins in the missionary God who purposed to fully restore humanity and creation. It was confirmed in his incarnation in Jesus Christ and through the apostolic message. 'At its most basic Integral Mission simply means "having it all". We want to worship and pray and preach and witness and serve and care. God put these things together and we should never have let them become separated.'[5]

When Christians fail to keep these aspects of God's mission together by selectively reducing them to suit their beliefs, an unbiblical dualism results. God's mission cannot be reduced to either/or; as his children, we should not offer either/or options to the world.

'BEING' IS CENTRAL

Our understanding of mission helps us live for the glory of God. We have a holistic vision of the Kingdom of God's impact on lives and communities. As salt that preserves and light that illuminates the world of need around us, we are called to proclaim the message of salvation.

Speaking to the Bangkok 2008 gathering of the World Evangelical Alliance's Evangelism Theology Commission, Justin Thacker called for a focus on 'being' the church instead of emphasising the activities of the church. It is not about separating and labelling activities as one type or the other and then ensuring a healthy mixture of both. Rather, it is about being the people of God in a world in need.[6]

René Padilla, Melba Maggay, and David Westlake of the Micah Network would agree:

> On the whole, our mission involves being, doing and saying what we are called to be, to do and to say as citizens of the Kingdom of God. It should not be narrowly understood as having to do merely with evangelism or social action, but with all of what it means to bear witness to the reign of Jesus in every dimension of life.[7]

'Christian' has too often become a great noun and a bad adjective because of the way we live and the way we respond to the need around us. How often do we say one thing and live the other, speaking of the love of God yet failing to demonstrate it?

CONSIDERING OUR MOTIVES

'How big is our gospel?' asks Christopher J.H. Wright. 'If our good news is about God's redemption, then the question moves on to, how big is our understanding of redemption?'[8] Understanding the magnitude and scope of God's redemptive plan can greatly help us respond to needs around us. Broadly speaking, in any disaster people need humanitarian assistance to help alleviate their suffering. Beneficiaries of our intervention programs also need God's salvation. Those responding to these situations have various motives, including the following:

Ecclesiological reasons:
Even in settings of relief and community development efforts, I have met missionaries sent by their churches to propagate their denomination. A danger is that we could focus on expanding our denominations rather than the growth of God's Kingdom.

Soteriological reasons:
Romans 10:13 offers a wonderful promise: Anyone who calls on the name of the Lord will be saved. The term 'anyone' is an inclusive invitation, open to all people from every tribe, nation, and language group. The condition to be saved is that they must call on Jesus. But people must go and tell them about the Saviour for them to believe, call on his name, and be saved.

This soteriological motivation is good, but it focuses on humanity. Should not all that God does be primarily for his own glory? When we respond to needs around us, we must be aware of the spiritual need that exists among the people or community we work with and respond accordingly. It is important we do not use humanitarian aid to lure them into Christianity. People who are 'hooked in' will easily fall away because their faith in Jesus is not based on a deep conviction of who Jesus is.

In my ten years of helping people in Sri Lanka and Greece, I have realised that the people and communities we serve know who we are; they respect our faith. Many are spiritually seeking and conscious about God. Spiritual conversation will come up as we serve and love them. When it does, we must be prepared and not ashamed to talk about Jesus (1 Pet. 3:15). Our zeal to share the gospel

Principle 4

must come with wisdom: discussing, learning, and asking questions about their religion to provoke their thinking, instead of arguing.

Humanitarian need is real:
Our response during a humanitarian crisis must be sincerely done out of the desire to alleviate suffering. During my work in Sri Lanka after the 2004 tsunami—and in Greece during the recent refugee crisis—I came across highly-paid workers motivated by money, not compassion.

As Christians, we are sent by God to be his hands and feet. We obey the call of God and go because of but not limited to these reasons:

We acknowledge that genuine need exists:
As Christian workers we must acknowledge that the people we are going to assist are genuinely in need. Understanding their suffering is essential in crafting an appropriate response.

We genuinely care:
I have learned that I can give food to homeless people yet not really love them. I always ask myself, 'Would I eat the food I am giving out?' If the answer is 'no' then I should not serve it.

We acknowledge that suffering is multidimensional:
In order to help we must learn to map out people's conditions. Most of the time, their real need may differ from what we assume. Wrong assumptions will not address their felt needs. Secondly, because suffering is multidimensional, we will not have all the answers. Thus it is important to partner with others to cover other areas while we discern an intervention programme that we can get involved in.

We are motivated by genuine love and compassion:
Agape love is unconditional. We do not feed people because we expect anything in return. We respond to their need because these are people whom God loves, and he created them in his image and likeness.

God's glory:
'Worship God,' declares Psalm 100 and countless other Bible passages. 'Bring my sons and daughters from afar,' God calls in Isaiah 43:6–7, 'everyone who is called by my name, whom I created for my glory…'

Following the writing of Christopher Wright, the mission of the church is only possible because God has a mission that it participates in. God's mission is for his own glory.[9]

Our motivation should be to glorify God: Father, Son and Holy Spirit. God's redemptive work covers every aspect of humanity. It cannot be reduced only to evangelism; regenerated beings will bring worship and glory to God in every aspect of their lives, including words and deeds.

SIGNS OF THE KINGDOM

In his opening chapter, Jonathan Williams explored the concept of the Kingdom of God and how an understanding of the Kingdom affects our service. Part of God's action of ruling and reigning is the redemption of his creation through Jesus, gathering people to himself so that they will reflect his character to those around them.

While the Kingdom is 'now and not yet', a sign of the Kingdom's presence is that we serve and meet needs as Jesus did because people are needy. We serve to help alleviate suffering. The signs of the Kingdom include people being transformed through the power of the cross.

When we respond to humanitarian needs around us, some people will respond by turning to Christ, but many will not—at least not within the duration of our programme intervention. We should not perceive a lack of evident spiritual response as failure. Rather, we are called to serve faithfully and trust God for the fruit.

> *Some years ago, I was involved in running a homeless and marginalised feeding programme in Athens through a local church. Each day, about 150–200 people from many nationalities would come and take food. Eventually a drop-in centre was opened, and we would hang out with the people. We had tea and coffee and made sandwiches for the guests.*
>
> *We got to know their names and made friends with many. Ioanis was a regular guest. He had a temper and felt that we owed him or that he deserved our services. I had numerous arguments with him and got to the point that I prayed that he would stop coming. While praying one day, I felt challenged to say some nice things about him. It was a struggle but eventually I did. It changed the way I talked and related to him.*
>
> *One winter, my young daughter and I brought a gas heater to the run-down house where he was living. My daughter met Ioanis and they exchanged a few words.*

Principle 4

A few days later, Ioanis showed up at the feeding programme with some bananas. He handed me the fruit and said, 'These are for your daughter.' It was very hard for me to accept them because he used the money that he earned by sitting on the roadside to buy my daughter bananas.

Although Ioanis came to a few Bible studies, he has not, to my knowledge, made a commitment to follow Christ. However, his attitudes and behaviour have changed. We trust God that in time he will make a commitment to follow Christ.

In our organisations, we set goals and strategies, and we work hard to archive these goals. Our aim is to impact as many people as possible; we call them 'our beneficiaries'. It is good to be intentional, yet we run the danger of making people our project goals, represented by the number of people we assist or hope to assist. These individuals can become merely our statistics.

During the 2018 consultation that gave rise to this book, we discussed change and our desire to contribute to positive impact. My colleague Cameron Willett expressed his distaste for numbers-focused attitudes and programme approaches. 'We don't want to count heads,' he said, 'but we can intentionally look at change, the kind of change that really is occurring. We might not be able to count people coming to faith, but we can observe and report on the change.'

The sign of the Kingdom is more than the number of people professing to follow Christ; it also means changes in lifestyle, behaviour, and attitude.

The sign of the Kingdom is not only about non-Christians turning to Christ. Instead, it includes the impact those of us who serve experience when we encounter the people we work with.

Humanity is created to bring worship to God through our lives. Those who know him are also called to go forth and preach the goodness about the Kingdom of God to the people still living in darkness so that they too can turn to Jesus and glorify God with their lives. Beyond words, those who know him are also called to demonstrate the love of God to the people around them.

As we embrace, experience, and express a holistic gospel, we are freed from defending either proclamation or demonstration and freed also from judging others. Often, those we seek to help and serve are quicker to evaluate our integrity and how we live and treat each other than we ourselves are. Imitating Jesus' way of life does not spring from conferences or papers, helpful as they may be; it happens as we together decide daily in every situation, seen and unseen, to do so. 'So if the Son sets you free, you will be free indeed' (John 8:36).

ENDNOTES

[1] 'History: World Council of Churches', accessed 18 February 2020, https://www.oikoumene.org/en/what-we-do/cwme/history.
[2] 'The Wheaton Declaration' (Wheaton, IL: Evangelical Missions Information Service, 1966), https://missionexus.org/the-wheaton-declaration/.
[3] 'The Lausanne Covenant', (Lausanne, Switzerland: 1 August 1974), https://www.lausanne.org/content/covenant/lausanne-covenant.
[4] Lausanne Committee, 'Evangelism and Social Responsibility: An Evangelical Commitment (LOP 21)' (Grand Rapids: The International Consultation on the Relationship Between Evangelism and Social Responsibility, 1982), https://www.lausanne.org/content/lop/lop-21.
[5] René Padilla, Melba Maggay, and David Westlake, 'Basic Introduction to Integral Mission' (Micah Network Integral Mission Initiative), accessed 19 February 2020, https://www.micahnetwork.org/sites/default/files/doc/library/basicintroductiontointegralmission_imi-fdn-001.pdf.
[6] Justin Thacker, 'A Holistic Gospel: Some Biblical, Historical and Ethical Considerations', *Evangelical Review of Theology* 33, no. 3 (July 2009), 5, 8.
[7] Padilla, Maggay, and Westlake, 'Basic Introduction to Integral Mission'.
[8] Christopher J. H. Wright, *The Mission of God: Unlocking the Bible's Grand Narrative* (Downers Grove: IVP Academic, 2006), 265.
[9] Wright, *The Mission of God*, 2006, 62.

ETHICAL EVANGELISM: INTEGRITY, TRUTH, TIMING, AND GRACE

Mark Galpin

Central to our lives and service is integrity, which is the basis of trust. Trust must be earned; it should not be presumed. A colleague in Central Asia observed, 'If people can trust you in what they see—how you work, what you do, how you change their lives—they are open to trust you and listen to stories of Jesus and how he can change their lives.' Beyond building trust with the community served, discussing the situation in his native Sri Lanka following the 2004 Boxing Day tsunami, Ajith Fernando emphasised the value of building trust with the authorities. At times, he wrote, it may be wiser 'to show the love of Christ by our actions and wait for other opportunities to explain fully the supreme way in which that love was expressed in Christ'.[1]

KINGDOM PERSPECTIVES AND TIMING

Are there times, then, when the verbal proclamation of the gospel is inappropriate and can do more harm than good? The answer depends on our understanding of salvation, of mission, and indeed of what 'the gospel' is. Is our aim purely to get as many individuals as possible to verbalise a commitment to Jesus? If so, then we might conclude: no; we must at all times and in all situations proclaim. Or is our call to join what God is doing in extending his Kingdom, recognising that both individuals coming to genuine faith and changes at the community and societal level are involved? These questions, and our answers, overlap with issues covered in Chapters 1–4 regarding the Kingdom of God and how we enter it, the nature of integral mission, and our desire to glorify Jesus Christ. A Kingdom perspective gives us a more holistic approach to mission and recognises that there may be times when, for the sake of God's Kingdom, proclamation needs to be postponed or left to others.

Vinoth Ramachandra observes that some people understand integral mission simply as doing both social action and proclamation at the same time. This creates tension, he says, for those who are working in contexts of human suffering.[2] Why?

Because in these contexts open proclamation can easily be, or be seen to be, coercive. Similar to the experiences David Greenlee recounts in Chapter 2, the timing and method of combining proclamation with meeting needs may send the implicit message that '[w]e will only continue to provide this service to you if you respond to the message we are proclaiming'. Even if a situation is not life-threatening, doing what your guest and benefactor asks you to do may simply be seen as the polite thing to do. People therefore feel forced to convert—or give the pretence of doing so—or to risk losing the aid they are receiving. Either way, in line with what David Lim has written (quoted by Greenlee in Chapter 2), the desire to convert in these situations is often not genuine. It does not come from an adequate understanding of the gospel, has not been made freely, and in the case of vulnerable individuals, may lead to significant negative impacts on the individual and community for which they are not well prepared.

However, sensitivity to the 'implicit messages' of our work can lead us to hide the fact that we are Christian or become too shy to share 'the hope that is within us' (1 Pet. 3:15) when suffering people themselves take the initiative to express a genuine interest. Suffering and vulnerable people have spiritual needs that organisations committed to holistic practice should be ready to meet or enable others to meet when they are requested to do so by those they are serving.

PROSELYTISATION AND UNHELPFUL PERCEPTIONS

What we consider to be appropriate sharing of our faith in these contexts may be described by others with the loaded word 'proselytism', a word many evangelicals associate with 'the abuse of people's freedom and the distortion of the gospel of grace by means of coercion, deception, manipulation, and exploitation'.[3] Unfortunately, in many contexts, external actors (including governments, donors, journalists, and local community leaders) suspect all Christian faith-based organisations of involvement in unethical proselytisation, which can lead to unnecessary obstacles for Christian service. Our response to this should not be to compromise our identity or gospel mandate but to sensitively engage and be scrupulously ethical in all our behaviour.

Ethical Evangelism

Responding to a Disaster

In the immediate aftermath of the Nepal earthquakes of 2015, many Christian organisations came to the country to provide relief. At a meeting of Christian relief agencies I attended, one organisational representative shared that their efforts were going well, but they were, as he put it, 'finding it a challenge to integrate evangelism with our relief distributions'.

Being one of the few in the room with more than a few weeks' experience in Nepal, I responded very strongly, making it clear that in no circumstances should they be trying to integrate evangelism with their relief. Why did I feel so strongly about this? I was very aware that in Nepal it is a very common accusation levelled at Christian agencies that they are 'proselytising' and coercing people to become Christians. Post-earthquake, the government was watching very closely for this. As Gabriel Markus describes in Chapter 4, recounting the experience of evangelical churches serving refugees in Greece, any hint of proselytism would have damaged the reputation not just of the organisation directly involved but potentially of all other Christians. It would have brought a negative impact on the perception of the gospel itself, and most likely have resulted in the banning of all Christian involvement in relief and reconstruction efforts, reducing the aid and support that was so desperately needed.

The local church in Nepal had taken a very clear stance that this was a time to meet people's immediate physical needs and not to engage in proclamation. In doing this, they were confident that they were, in this situation, appropriately bearing witness to the love Christ has for all people of whatever faith. The time for proclamation would come; this was the time for demonstration.

The organisation mentioned had no understanding of the context. Their approach was driven by a need to feel that they were doing 'integral mission' themselves in this situation. This stemmed from a restricted and limited understanding of God's Kingdom. As such, they did more harm than good.

Insights from Others

The Cape Town Commitment opens its section on 'living the love of Christ among people of other faiths', stating:

> We are called to share good news in evangelism, but not to engage in unworthy proselytizing. Evangelism, which includes persuasive rational argument following the example of the Apostle Paul, is 'to make an honest and open statement of the gospel which leaves the hearers entirely free to make up their own minds about it. We wish to be sensitive to those of other faiths, and we reject any approach that seeks to force conversion on them. Proselytizing, by contrast, is the attempt to compel others to become 'one of us', to 'accept our religion', or indeed to 'join our denomination'.
>
> ...We commit ourselves to be scrupulously ethical in all our evangelism. Our witness is to be marked by 'gentleness and respect, keeping a clear conscience.' We therefore reject any form of witness that is coercive, unethical, deceptive, or disrespectful.[4]

But how do we know when we are being unethical? Much helpful work has been done on defining the boundaries and standards for ethical witness. The ecumenical document 'Christian Witness in a Multi-Religious World: Recommendations for Conduct' sets out a basis for Christian witness and key principles that should be adhered to, particularly in interreligious contexts.[5] The Oslo Coalition on Freedom of Religion and Belief facilitated a consultative process among people from a wide range of faith backgrounds and also those of no religious faith, all of whom were committed to the human right of freedom of religion—including the promotion of one's own religion. The resulting document includes guidelines for missionary activities and charity work. Charities should be transparent about their religious affiliation, and while charity is an end in itself and should not be regarded as a means to convert people, it is appropriate and permissible to respond to genuine enquiries about the organisation's affiliation. Specific guidelines for evangelism among vulnerable groups such as children and refugees are also provided, emphasising the need to ensure that steps taken to change religious identity are genuine and not coerced.[6]

In contrast to the Cape Town Commitment above, Elmer Thiessen argues that proselytisation (in the formal sense of the word, propagation of one's faith) in itself is not unethical. Any type of 'marketing activity' is a type of proselytisation[7] and can be done in unethical ways. He then goes on to set out key summary criteria for an ethical approach to proselytisation or evangelism that includes:

- Ensuring the dignity and worth of the person(s) being evangelised
- Showing concern for the whole person and all of his/her needs
- Refraining from the use of physical force or psychological coercion, or inducements of any kind
- Providing information for a person to make a rational decision
- Seeking to tell the truth about the religion being advocated, as well as other religions
- Is characterised by humility
- Treating people holding differing beliefs with love and respect and being sensitive to their culture.[8]

NO SHADOW ON GOD'S GRACE

At its heart, the gospel is a message of grace. No one who understands this will seek to 'coerce' someone else into faith. However, our lack of understanding of the context that we are serving in and a misplaced and individualistic interpretation of integral or holistic mission—a belief that we need to do it all, now—can result in efforts that 'cast a shadow on the grace of God', as expressed by a student of mine who had been subject to such efforts. Rather, we must ensure that we are motivated by love at all times, that we seek to understand the context that we are working in, and that we see our role from the wider perspective of joining in with others with what God is doing.

ENDNOTES

[1] Ajith Fernando, 'Evangelism and Tsunami Relief', *Leighton Ford Ministries* (23 June 2014), https://www.leightonfordministries.org/2014/06/23/evangelism-and-tsunami-relief/.

[2] Vinoth Ramachandra, 'What Is Integral Mission?' (Micah Network Integral Mission Initiative),

https://www.micahnetwork.org/sites/default/files/doc/library/whatisintegralmission_imi-the-001.pdf.
[3] A. Scott Moreau, Harold Netland, and Charles E. van Engen (eds), *Evangelical Dictionary of World Missions* (Grand Rapids: Baker, 2000), s.v. proselytism.
[4] 'The Cape Town Commitment' (Cape Town: Lausanne Movement, 2010), https://www.lausanne.org/content/ctc/ctcommitment.
[5] World Council of Churches, Pontifical Council for Interreligious Dialogue, and World Evangelical Alliance, 'Christian Witness in a Multi-Religious World: Recommendations for Conduct' (2011), http://www.worldevangelicals.org/pdf/1106Christian_Witness_in_a_Multi-Religious_World.pdf.
[6] Ingunn Folkestad Breistein, 'Missionary Activities and Human Rights: Recommended Ground Rules for Missionary Activities' (Oslo: Oslo Coalition on Freedom of Religion or Belief, 2009), https://www.jus.uio.no/smr/english/about/programmes/oslocoalition/docs/groundrules_folkestad_breiestein.pdf.
[7] Elmer Thiessen, *The Ethics of Evangelism: A Philosophical Defence of Ethical Proselytizing and Persuasion* (Paternoster: Milton Keynes, 2011), 16.
[8] Thiessen, *The Ethics of Evangelism*, 2011, chap. 7,8.

Principle 5:
Prayer, Spiritual Warfare, and Change

Holly Steward

As a choral and orchestral musician with a university degree in English, I was not the obvious candidate to be involved in community development along the shores of Lake Tanganyika. Yet God in his providence (and possibly sense of humour) took me to Zambia, first as a teacher for a missionary family and, in turn, working under African leadership to coordinate Zambian disciple-makers working within fishing communities among several vulnerable groups in society.

I knew that I was created by a good God who knows me, cares for me, and has a purpose for me. What I had not considered was the incredible difference this assurance makes when contrasted to those without hope. This realisation came to me during my first visit to a remote fishing village whose people's lives were rooted in animism and ancestor worship.

What I saw was fear and hopelessness in their eyes but also in how they interacted with each other. Neighbours assumed that they were being cursed by each other. Every detail of life was seen as a potential spiritual threat. Their foundational beliefs were centred on good and bad spirits: appeasing the good ones through rituals protects you from the bad. In some cases, people did find improvement; the evil one has limited power for apparent healing and improvement, but this leads to increased dependence on and manipulation by witch doctors—and ever deeper hopelessness.

Efforts by Christians to reach this area date back over 120 years to the visits of David Livingstone and later teams of the London Missionary Society. The ruins of a stone church building they built are symbolic of the sparse fruit left from those days: every Christian ministry that has since attempted to work here has failed.

In 2006, when our first workers moved to the Zambian border on the Lake Tanganyika shoreline, they heard of the region's reputation for spiritual darkness: blood sacrifices of both humans and animals were at the core of rituals performed for generations. When I joined them in 2008, I realised that most of the team's work had been, wisely, to build a spiritual foundation.

We were struck by the lack of food, clothing, basic health care, and education in these communities. Eventually, our approach did include health, education, and teaching about efficient use of natural resources. But it was vividly apparent that transformative change had to first occur within their spiritual core. In one village, an American built a school and a clinic. He confided to us his frustration that, in spite of such significant investment in the community, the destructive behaviours of the people did not change.

How does lasting change come about? Our team had begun with the overarching truth that perfect love casts out fear (1 John 4:18). Realising that our battle is not against flesh and blood (Eph. 6:12), and rather than focusing on those important healthcare and well-being activities, our team prioritised prayer walks and Scripture proclamation. Three days a week, we prayer-walked through the villages from 6 to 7 a.m., reading Scripture verses aloud. This faithful discipline was a tangible, consistent contrast to the practices typical of the community.

MORE THAN CONQUERORS

The words 'spiritual warfare' conjure up contrasting images, even to those who consider it a real part of their lives and service. We might think of serious injuries and accidents as spiritual attacks. Perhaps we think of demonic rituals and curses. Less often, we think of the struggle against corrupted structures of power and the pervasive power of deception that continue to crush people and keep them alienated from God.

Spiritual opposition may also come in the humdrum of daily life. A colleague in Asia wrote:

We feel that spiritual opposition comes in waves, and often in ways we do not expect. We have not had opposition from the religious establishment or local government, who actually welcome our work because they see tangible benefits for the children and families we work with. But I find it comes in subtle ways into our community development team, through discouragement, misunderstanding and conflict, illness, visa issues, and other frustrations, which I feel want to come at us 'from within'.

I have seen breakthroughs after a dramatic exorcism of a man who performed blood rituals his whole life—perhaps the image some hold when thinking about 'spiritual warfare' among the least reached. However, progress towards a loving community also occurs in the daily life choices of a husband carrying a bucket of water for his wife (a shockingly selfless act in his context). When another man cared for an orphaned nephew as if he was a son, rather than a second-class slave waiting for scraps after a family meal, his actions spoke loudly—as did the changed behaviour of other

Principle 5

families as they began to demonstrate such counter-cultural acts of love. These reflect the subtle aspects of spiritual victories that lead to transformation and freedom.

Whatever the manifestation, subtle or overt, the consistent image is that we are in a battle, often seeing ourselves as on the defensive. However, thanks to Jesus, we are on the winning side of this battle that has already been won! As mysterious or unsettling as spiritual attacks may be, we are 'more than conquerors' (Rom. 8:37), not only protected but effective warriors from whom evil must flee.

ENTERING A LAKE TANGANYIKA FISHING COMMUNITY

When planning to work in a new community, it is of paramount importance to consider spiritual warfare in our strategy. We know we will encounter spiritual attacks when treading on ground where the enemy has ruled unchallenged. How can we enter fully shielded by the armour of God? How can walking in the Spirit daily keep us on the offensive? How will our presence in the community reveal the Kingdom of God?

As described in Luke 4:18–19 (quoting Isa. 61:1–3), Jesus came to bind up the brokenhearted, proclaim freedom for the captives, and release prisoners from darkness. In response to questions from John the Baptist's disciples asking if he was the one who was to come, Jesus responded, 'The blind receive sight, the lame walk, those who have leprosy are cleansed, the deaf hear, the dead are raised, and the good news is proclaimed to the poor' (Luke 7:22). In my experience in Zambia, the first sign of a community in bondage to the enemy is fear; elsewhere it might be seen in hopelessness, greed, violence, or self-centredness. However, a follower of Jesus walking into such a community will naturally radiate a love that is like light in the darkness (Matt. 5:14–16). The Kingdom of God breaks out when Jesus is revealed!

The Zambian missionaries who moved into these villages initially did not only distribute material necessities but focused on showing love. They played with neglected children (not customary for adults there). The homes of Jesus followers attracted people where, instead of accusation and suspicion, they found a welcome and acceptance. Soon, villagers discovered that they could bring family members who were ill to the 'missionary' for prayer instead of paying the witch doctor for a ritual. These traditional healers used sincere but misguided efforts, such as cutting the sick person and putting herbs in the wound, often resulting in infection; there were also instances of witch doctors forcing people to drink kerosene or applying concentrated bleach to a wound.

We observed that the Holy Spirit's active presence was accentuated in these places where the people's faith in the supernatural was already strong. They needed only to shift their belief from expecting that curses would make them sick or hungry to believing that the Creator God wants to heal them. Many were healed and delivered through prayer. People began to see the clear choice between faith in God and the rituals of the witch doctor, as happened in a village where the headman's wife had been a witch doctor but had become a believer, a demonstration of Jesus' power for deliverance.

In that village *Gloria**, the wife of a village fisherman, came to *Alfred**, one of our team, because of multiple miscarriages. During each of her previous pregnancies, she dreamed of a knife attacking her and would lose the baby the following day. When she came to Alfred, the woman was pregnant again; she begged him to pray for a healthy baby. One day soon after, Gloria came to Alfred distressed because she had again dreamed of the knife attack. Alfred prayed for Gloria, who later delivered her first healthy baby. Later, Alfred himself had a disturbing dream of a knife attacking him, but he woke up, rebuked the demon in Jesus' name, laughed at the enemy's attempt to scare him, and continued his sleep in peace.

In those early days, it was encouraging to see people healed and delivered from bondage to blood sacrifices. However, the pattern of new believers in Jesus coming under significant spiritual attack also became quickly apparent. The core Lake Tanganyika team was committed to fasting every Monday, year after year, as this work was launched around the lakeshore villages. We had a sense that the weekly fasting and prayer as a team was the most effective way to stand against the attacks on the new disciples.

With the day-to-day work in the villages, there was no clear line between spiritual teaching and physical help. Responding with food, supplies, and building materials after much of a village was wiped out in a landslide spoke as clearly to the people as an evening talk under a mango tree about whether to trust in a sacrifice ritual

Principle 5

or prayer. My Western way of separating the spiritual and physical components of life was irrelevant among these people.

Sometimes it felt like the new believers slipped back more frequently than they grew in their faith. However, in every village there are men who testify that because of their new faith they have stopped getting drunk and beating their wives every night. One home was referred to by the village as being its own radio, because the screams of the wife as she was beaten were heard every night. When this man repented and stopped the abuse, the whole village noticed. As the spiritual battle was waged, patterns of behaviour started to change; the community began to see hope for change from what had long been considered 'normal', even if harmful. These changes were not the result merely of teaching, even from the Bible; they only came as spiritual victories were won through prayer.

THE SPIRIT WITH YOU IS MORE POWERFUL

Many of our team members were Zambians with limited skills and education. In one village on Lake Tanganyika, we discovered that the headman—who was also the witch doctor—saw something more in them. 'The Spirit that is with you is more powerful than the ones that we have in us,' he told them. 'Our charms and rituals do not work anymore now that the Spirit in you is in our village.'

One of the clearest indicators of a spiritual power encounter is in the mindset shift of trusting in witchcraft versus God's provision. All men in these villages survive by fishing, mostly in teams on wooden boats with large nets. We learned that, when each of the hundreds of boats on the lake had been launched, human sacrifice was carried out. This reveals why the bondage to fear and destruction is so strong: The enemy has been given permission to hold these people in bondage by their willing choice to shed blood. We were reminded repeatedly of our complete reliance on prayer and Scripture as the only way to stand against such a long-standing practice.

So we launched a fishing boat, commissioned with prayer, as the 'Good News'. As the villagers mocked, the 'Good News' fishing team announced that they would not rely on rituals for a good catch of fish. Over time, when the 'Good News' crew did catch fish, even sometimes when other boats had not, the community took notice. One villager described it to the village headman, who was part of the 'Good News' fishing crew, 'We have seen that you can catch fish without sacrificing. We make sacrifices for so many other things in our daily lives; maybe we don't need to make sacrifices for those either.'

Even in villages where only a few people became believers, the mind and heart transformation impacts the overall community. Even a vague sense of a Creator God helps a people learn to value their physical environment and resources. In one village, always littered with paper and plastic, people gradually started to bury or burn rubbish. Fishermen used to waste any extra fish caught, beyond what could be sold or consumed that day—but the longer the presence of the Holy Spirit was there, the more likely they were to adopt habits like drying and preserving the fish for another day.

THREE KEY PRACTICES

I have found three practices to be key in winning spiritual victories: rejoicing, proclaiming God's word, and repenting.

Rejoicing

The enemy gains power when people choose to make blood sacrifices to the spirits, but Otto Koning learned how the powers of darkness are dispelled at times in the presence of worship and rejoicing. Koning became a missionary among tribes in the jungles of what is now Papua, Indonesia. In the inspiring 'The Pineapple Story' series, he recounts lessons learned as his wife and he served among tribes and villages that previously had little, if any, chance to hear and understand the gospel. A painful encounter helped him learn the importance of rejoicing (Jas. 1:2–4) as a weapon of spiritual warfare, summarised here.

> *While crossing a jungle swamp with a few helpers, Koning walked too close to a hornets' nest. Badly stung and in great pain, he started to panic, knowing he could die from the poison. But even in the pain, God was there and Koning sensed his presence. 'And I said God, what do I do? And I heard one word in a clear voice in my mind; "Rejoice." I said, "No! I am in severe pain on this trail, and the last thing I feel like doing is to rejoice!"' But he did. He stood up on a log and said, 'God I praise you, I give you thanks for the hornets,' words spoken as an act of will, not of feeling; out of obedience, not understanding. But he says, 'As we start rejoicing in tribulation that is when God begins to move on our behalf.'*

Koning and his helpers continued to their destination village. The villagers were aware of Koning's deep suffering from the hornet attack suffered on his way to visit them. Telling each other, 'He must have a very important message to tell us!', they listened attentively as one of the young men spoke to them of Jesus. As a result, Koning says, 'This started the seed of the gospel in that village, in that tribe.'

Looking back on this experience, Koning reminds us that 'When we start rejoicing in the midst of tribulation, that's when God starts to move on our behalf. We get much more done rejoicing and surrendering than begging and pleading...I started to rejoice. And I saw that is a powerful weapon of our spiritual warfare.' [1]

Proclaiming God's word

Along with rejoicing, proclaiming scripture aloud has a profound impact in the spiritual atmosphere because God's word is powerful; it is alive and active, sharper than any double-edged sword (Heb. 4:12). Knowing this, during the first decade of our community work at Lake Tanganyika, our team read aloud the entire Bible two different times, standing in the ruins of the stone church founded by David Livingstone's mission contacts a century before.

Repenting

This is the third key element in spiritual warfare as we seek transformation. The area around our team's Lake Tanganyika base is known for its barren landscapes; there is little wildlife, and even after years of living there, team members could not remember hearing birds sing. Just opposite our lakeshore base lies an uninhabited island owned by the regional chief, dedicated as a place for sacrifices he offers.

Building on the prayers raised by the team over several years, prayer warriors from South Africa, Tanzania, and several Zambian tribes prayed together for several days, lifting up their voices in worship to the Lord. They acknowledged their tribes had sinned by spilling human blood in sacrifice to false spirits. On behalf of their tribes, they repented of this bloodshed and accepted God's freedom and forgiveness. Those present experienced a sensation of a burden being lifted.

In the weeks after the prayer outreach, we began to see vividly coloured birds appear in our trees; they woke us in the morning with their songs. What a testimony to the power of repentance and worship in the presence of God! God is faithful to all his promises and longs to bring salvation and freedom to his people and all creation.

SUFFERING AND POWER: INSIGHTS FROM CENTRAL ASIA

Suffering is common to human experience, something community development workers face frequently. Many traditional religions explain suffering as the acts of spiritual beings, often provoked by curses performed by enemies. Some Muslims see suffering as a result of curses or 'the evil eye', but for Muslim friends of a colleague in Central Asia, suffering is often a form of punishment. In dealing with illness or the disability of a child, everything that happens is simply 'the will of Allah'.

To deal with suffering, many Central Asian Muslims turn to those who can mediate and help them find spiritual solutions. Needing power, they turn to power people, power places, and power rituals that connect at *mazars* (mausoleums or shrines), where a holy person may say prayers and recitations over the persons in need, instructing them to perform certain rituals that may include animal sacrifice.

Reflecting further on these ideas, my colleague wrote:

> *Spiritual warfare is a reality. In our project for children with disabilities, we realise that you cannot separate physical and medical reasons for the disability from the spiritual reasons seen by the people here. Solutions must address both physical and spiritual causes.*
>
> *As we welcome and show love to these children, we are declaring to the spiritual realm that these children are not cursed or rejected by God. Many mothers also believe that the disability is a spiritual punishment for their own sins. Through counselling, we clearly explain that the God we believe in is a God of love, who loves the mother and the child, and this is not the way God chooses to punish sin. Through such conversations many mothers burst into tears; this is something they have never heard before.*
>
> *Since prayer is a part of daily life here we also offer to pray for the mother. Mostly they are quite surprised at the way we pray: 'You pray to God like he is personal. You talk to him. And you can ask him to help. We don't pray in this way.' The form of prayer they have learned is like a recitation, 'May God do this or this; may he help'. They have never heard God being spoken to in such a personal way. This is a key way that our work with families of children with disabilities demonstrates love, a loving God and how we can relate and talk to this loving God through prayer.*

Principle 5

TRUE FASTING, OPEN DOORS

In Central Asia, because disability is seen as a spiritual curse, children with disabilities are kept at home. Many mothers and families show very deep love and care for their child at home, but going out in public can be traumatic for the child and the family: people stare, point at the child, or ask in a pitying way what is wrong. Until recently, children with disabilities were not seen in public, parks, or play areas. Many never had the opportunity to go to school or play with other children on the street.

These attitudes and behaviours are a form of discrimination and oppression linked with a wrong spiritual belief of what causes disability. Education and good examples may help, but we must also recognise the spiritual warfare involved. The spiritual disciplines of prayer and fasting will be part of our response. As recorded in Isaiah 58, true fasting involves faithful lives; it can be seen in loosing chains of injustice, setting the oppressed free, and caring for the poor and hungry. In this light, working with children with disabilities in Central Asia is in itself an act of fasting.

As may be the case in other least-reached settings, community development like this project may also be a door opener, lending credibility to Jesus followers even in spiritually harsh and conservative areas, a theme explored in other chapters of this book.

DEALING WITH WEBS OF SIN

Spiritual warfare may involve dramatic exorcism and deliverance from overt spiritual powers. In some cases, our Spirit-filled presence in and of itself is a projection of God's power among the weak and needy (Psa. 82:4), of his light shining into darkness (Isa. 58:10).

Jayakumar Christian recognises the spiritual aspects associated with powerlessness, poverty, and the related webs of sin,[2] themes I have considered above. Breaking such oppression requires a multidimensional approach: practical help, physical explanations, but also a demonstration that God loves them and can break the power of evil spirits.

In other settings, sin's impact pervades society in less overt ways, such as corruption, as touched on by Martin Allaby in his reflection on that theme later in this book. Walter Wink describes such evil, systemic powers as real, not 'mere personifications' of an evil concept.

> *When a particular Power becomes idolatrous, placing itself above God's purposes for the good of the whole, then that Power becomes demonic. The church's task is to unmask this idolatry and recall the Power to their created purposes in the world – 'so that the Sovereignties and Powers should learn only now, through the Church, how comprehensive God's wisdom really is' (Eph. 3:10 JB).[3]*

Writing from a country plagued by corruption, a business and development practitioner observes:

> *My workers (not yet believers in Jesus) are getting used to and appreciating the work atmosphere. They love the project concept. At each new stage or step forward, I or my business partner pray publicly, giving God glory for each completed step and asking for wisdom, protection, revelation, and finances to move forward. The workers are investing themselves into the work in the hope that we can start production. We do, however, often remind them that the mechanics of creating a profitable enterprise is only the first step. Once we are operational the real, spiritual battle will begin. These men are well aware of the enormity of evil in a society ruled by corruption. May salvation come and faith be born in these men. I believe our actions in the physical world can be projections of our faith into the community and instruments (weapons?) in a spiritual war. Light has come into a dark place.*

Whether confronting the idolatry of power, dehumanizing cultural values, or the forces of bondage I encountered in Zambia, Wink's words are relevant to our theme of Jesus followers and community development among least-reached communities:

> *We must develop a fine-tuned sensitivity to what the ancients called 'the war in heaven.' It is the unseen clash of values and ideologies, of the spirituality of institutions and the will of God, of demonic factionalism and heavenly possibilities. The unique calling of the church in social change lies in making clear the dual nature of our task. We wrestle on two planes, the earthly and the heavenly.[4]*

REJOICE WITH THE HEAVENS!

As God builds his Kingdom here on Earth, we are heirs with Christ; if we endure, we will also reign with him (Rom. 8:17; 2 Tim. 2:12). While there will be moments of joy and victory, we will also experience opposition; we struggle not against merely human forces but also 'against the rulers, against the authorities, against the powers of this

Principle 5

dark world and against the spiritual forces of evil in the heavenly realms' (Eph. 6:12).

Victories in the spiritual realm may contribute to restoration in the environment around us. At times we will see deliverance, lives changed, even values and structures of society transformed. At other times we will be like the saints in the final verses of Hebrews 11; the world—seemingly in power as it pursued them—not worthy of them. Change may come in small steps, but it comes.

God's Kingdom has come; God's Kingdom is coming. It comes with salvation, with power, and with the authority of Jesus Christ, the Messiah. As God's Kingdom comes there is a battle with our furious enemy whose time is short. We need not fear, even though he accuses us; we triumph by the blood of the Lamb and by the word of our testimony, not loving our lives so much as to shrink from death. We rejoice with the heavens! (Rev. 12:10–12)

ENDNOTES

---

[1] Otto Koning, 'The Weapon of Rejoicing', Audio Session 12 of Bill Gothard and Otto Koning, *The Pineapple Story* (book originally published: Oak Brook, IL: Institute in Basic Life Principles, 1978) accessed 9 March 2020, https://embassymedia.com/media/session-12-weapon-rejoicing.
[2] Jayakumar Christian, *God of the Empty-Handed: Poverty, Power and the Kingdom of God*, 2nd Kindle (Brunswick East, Australia: Acorn Press, 2011), chap. 7.
[3] Walter Wink, *Naming the Powers: The Language of Power in the New Testament* (Philadelphia: Fortress Press, 1984), 5, 136.
[4] Wink, *Naming the Powers*, 1984, 130.

Principle 6: Caring for Creation as Worship, Witness, and Obedience

Robert Sluka

I received an email from a team seeking to bless a least-reached Muslim community by helping protect seagrass beds that, when healthy, can provide abundant food; theirs were not. The team, which is also seeking to see a community of Jesus followers develop, was unsure whether their efforts were in accord with current ecological understanding. Their sending agency did not have the capacity or expertise to support this aspect of their Kingdom work. Could I help them?

Earth's environment features heavily in current news and in the minds of many as one of the most, if not *the* most, important issue today. Secular sources inform us of the urgency in mitigating the devastating consequences of our poor stewardship. For example, a recent study showed that only four per cent of the total weight of all mammals on Earth are wild animals with the rest being humans (35 per cent) and livestock.[1] But why is this important to our exploration of community development among least-reached communities (CDLR) and the more traditional focus of missions on one species: *Homo sapiens*? What does creation care have to do with missions and particularly the interaction between community development, least-reached people, and the formation of new, vibrant churches?

I will not offer an apologetic for creation care as a Christian activity. Numerous introductory texts do this quite well.[2] Among evangelicals, an encouraging sign of changing attitudes is the joint Creation Care Network of the Lausanne Movement and the World Evangelical Alliance. The Lausanne Movement declared in its 2010 Cape Town Commitment that creation care is a gospel issue under the lordship of Jesus Christ.[3] A later meeting led to publication of *Creation Care and the Gospel*,[4] including case studies of creation care projects around the globe. Other sources of information include presentations at the 2018 'Creation Care at the Frontiers of Mission' conference hosted by Frontier Ventures (formerly US Center for World Mission).[5]

CREATION CARE: DEFINITION AND EXAMPLES

Creation care is not a theory of origins, nor does it presuppose any particular stance on 'how' God created the world. A Christian view starts with Genesis 1: 'In the beginning God...' The full range of Christian views regarding origins are compatible with creation care, which is synonymous with the secular term conservation. The roots of this word, though, are actually quite biblical; conservation means to serve with.[6] In the first creation narrative in Genesis, humans were created in God's image and, accordingly, tasked to care for his world. If we think of God as a despot who selfishly uses his creation just to please himself then we could conceivably do the same. However, we were made in the image of a loving, gentle, merciful, and gracious Father, so we need to exercise dominion in that image.

Creation care is as much an attitude as an activity. It helps us see the world as full of God's creatures and places he created to glorify himself. Understanding of place and the relationships between species and habitats is critical for developing creation care projects. It will not do to simply import ideas from elsewhere; all ideas must be adapted to the specific combination of climate, species, habitats, people, and cultures.

Principle 6, the theme of this chapter, states in part that 'our concern for creation is an act of obedience to God and participation in his work of reconciling all things to himself.' We are responsible to care for creation in our everyday lives and also corporately as mission communities. Creation care is an important principle at the intersection of the CDLR paradigm, but that can easily translate into supporting, praying for, and sending to the 'other' while our own daily actions directly or indirectly negatively impact those close to us and even that 'other'. For example, how we utilise energy impacts those nearby and far away through climate change. The food we serve and buy locally is at the end of a long chain of cursing or blessing: Where did that canned tuna come from, and how were those who fished it treated?[7] It is hypocrisy and folly to think that creation care only matters to those on the other side of the planet. We are all interconnected through wind, water, and food chains; what we do locally matters in that place, but it also impacts those far away.

A Rocha Australia's Board Chair shows how pertinent this can be, describing his team's experiences during the 2019 bushfires:

Principle 6

Directors and supporters of A Rocha Australia have faced the fear and uncertainty of fires bearing down on their community and homes. As we witness this ecological catastrophe, many have been involved in helping evacuees, providing comfort to the distraught and explaining the relevance of the Bible to the fires and Earth's climate emergency. We grieve and lament for lives lost, people made homeless, wildlife killed, farms charred, forests scorched, businesses destroyed. Although we are sad and exhausted we continue in the hope we have in Christ, knowing that God is reconciling all things to himself (Col. 1:20), committed to using and caring for his Creation (Gen. 2:15), and awaiting the renewal of his heavens and earth at Jesus' return.[8]

THE KINGDOM OF GOD EXTENDED TO ALL CREATION

Our worldview and ideas about the Kingdom of God often begin at the fall of man and end at the cross. Yet the Scripture starts with the creation, moves to the fall, the all-sufficient death and resurrection of Christ on the cross, and then on to the new creation with the Church occupying the space between the latter two markers in time and space. God declared the pre-human creation 'good' and tasked humanity with its care and service—a task not revoked after the fall. Sin impacted all of creation; throughout Scripture, God is concerned for non-human creation. The cross fixes all that was broken, including non-human creation. We see in Revelation 5 not only from every tribe, people, nation, and language but also 'every creature in heaven and on Earth and under the earth and on the sea' before God's throne praising him with the very same song (Rev. 5:13). A truly biblical view of the Kingdom of God must include all of creation in its theological and practical expressions.

Recent advances in mission have combatted the dualism and individualism that has permeated much of Christianity, particularly in the West. However, there remains a strong anthropocentrism that limits the Kingdom of God to humanity. Biblically, the Kingdom of God extends to all that he made. We should therefore think not only in terms of how we might bring God's Kingdom among people but to all creation (see Mark 16:15). The restoration and reconciliation of all places, including the many species and habitats besides *Homo sapiens*, are central to our calling as followers of Christ. Creation care is thus not simply a principle that helps us achieve the aims expressed in the CDLR process but a goal at the heart of the paradigm. In the diagram included in the Introduction, this idea could be represented either by another circle that aims to represent all non-human creation or by changing our understanding that our goals within missions not only apply to people but also to place.

THE CDLR MODEL: WHERE DOES CREATION CARE FIT?
I have argued above that creation care should have its own circle as co-equal with community development in a holistic model of the Kingdom of God. Working within the framework of the CDLR model helps us understand how it interacts with and can facilitate community development and the establishment of vibrant followers of Jesus among the least reached. I will first examine how creation care interacts with each of these topics and then look for the intersection of these three spaces, suggesting practical ways in which creation care can be integrated into our current mission activity.

Community Development
There has been a long interaction of creation care and development with various levels of goal congruence. Initially, conservation focused on excluding people, often forcefully, by creating protected areas with limited access. Practitioners were focused on non-human creation and the habitats that supported them. People were seen as the problem, causing declines in species and habitat quality. A relationship began to develop between the conservation and development disciplines, which explored people as part of the natural environment and recognised that the success of protected areas depended on support from local communities; what happened outside protected areas could be very detrimental to the species and habitats living inside them. A synergistic goal sought a win-win situation where communities benefit from the protection of nature, and nature itself is protected. There is a continuum among positions of practitioners as to how conservation and poverty alleviation/community development interact. Values and tools used vary depending on the understanding of this relationship.[9] Yet it is now recognised that often there are no win-win situations. A review of published literature on conservation measures aimed at poverty reduction identified only ten types of conservation projects that clearly demonstrated not only nature protection but clear benefits to communities.[10]

The history and literature of this relationship is rich and cannot be summarised here, but several points merit discussion in relation

Principle 6

to understanding how creation care fits within the CDLR model. Clearly the health of environments and the wellbeing of the communities who live in them are linked. The need for clean water, for example, is juxtaposed with wells and rivers contaminated by mining that expose communities to toxic levels of mercury or arsenic. Desertification—the process of dry, sandy areas overtaking pastureland and forest—reduces grazing areas and can force intergroup conflict over diminishing resources. Overfishing causes poor coastal fishermen to use more resources to go farther and fish deeper and usually results in lower quality species being available, reducing protein intake and economic gain.

One area increasingly explored is that of resilience as a bridge between conservation and development.[11] Resilience is applied to what practitioners now call socio-ecological systems, which indicate that social and ecological systems are intertwined and cannot be separated. Andrew Newsham and Shonil Bhagwat[12] use the framework of resilience proposed by Christophe Béné and colleagues, which I will also use, as it comes more clearly from development literature than ecological literature. They argue that 'resilience can be defined as the ability to deal with the impacts of adverse changes and shocks'.[13] Multiple aspects of this definition are explored by Newsham and Bhagwat and include the ability to buffer against impacts, the ability to return to a pre-shock condition, and the ability of communities to evolve or adapt. The picture here is of an economic or natural disaster 'shock' that causes a great disruption in a community, including its relationship to the natural environment. A resilient community will have more opportunities available if one economic stream is disrupted and will bounce back more quickly from a disaster.

Newsham and Bhagwat are worth quoting here in relation to this concept of resilience.

> *Because resilience is so rooted in the concept of the social-ecological system, it provides deep theoretical insights into the interconnections and interdependencies characterizing the relationship between conservation and development. It helps us to understand, in essence, why it is necessary to reconcile conservation imperatives with the demand for development. It allows us to see, in other words, how any development trajectory requires some level of conservation built into it, whilst the nature of what we want to*

conserve is fundamentally altered by the development trajectory that we choose.[14]

The authors present the 2004 Asian tsunami as an example of the impact of the state of local ecological systems on a community's ability to bounce back (i.e. resilience). They caution that resilience thinking is not a panacea, but it does help us to place concepts onto a framework that might help development practitioners more deeply to integrate conservation into their work.

Creation care and community development is one area most explored within the literature and practice. Dorothy Boorse's 'Loving the Least of These' offers a valuable place to start from a Christian perspective, linking our changing planet to issues of development, particularly among the poor.[15] A Rocha's work has had a strong focus on poverty alleviation alongside creation care, working on projects in Africa, Asia, and South America[16] as described on the A Rocha website. These illustrate further our Principle 6: 'Community development approaches that demonstrate good stewardship of the environment help promote the care of creation among the communities we serve.'

Vibrant Communities of Jesus Followers

While the focus of creation care organisations has not been to form fellowships out of their work, they often work through such fellowships. We can see how creation care could facilitate their formation. Further, it is youth who are calling us to take environmental issues seriously. In A Rocha, our centres are open to young people who care deeply about the environment and, sad to say, are through with the Church because of its lack of voice on the topic. Many who relate to God through nature and for whom this is a significant issue will never find a vibrancy of faith without these most important areas coming under the lordship of Jesus.

Research on fellowships that begin from followers of Islam becoming believers in Jesus indicates an important consideration: that resultant fellowships will often model the initial patterns of those who begin it.[17] One veteran missionary in Kenya writes of his experience this way:

> *Once carpeted by a lush cedar and African olive forest that fed streams out into the Rift Valley, many kilometers of the Kijabe escarpment now lie*

denuded of forest cover, and the streams have dried up. As my counterpart spoke with passion about the biblical foundations for creation stewardship and how we can honor Christ through caring for the environment, one member of the community, hearing this teaching for the first time, became obviously excited. With urgency he asked: 'Why is it that for all these decades the missionaries right here have never told us that God was concerned about how we managed the forests? Why have they just watched this destruction taking place?'[18]

While I want to be careful not to judge past endeavours where workers were not trained or knowledgeable about the role of the environment in missions and its impact on people and cultures, Kenyan Christians display the dualistic, anthropogenic focus that typifies much of Western Christian missions theology and practice.

If those seeking to start VCJF do not model creation care and its integration into fellowship life, it is unlikely that those fellowships will pursue those paths. We cannot, as many want to, start a fellowship and think that discipleship will result in a holistic outcome. Holism—integral mission—needs to be part of the focus of the fellowship from the outset, modelled by those who are helping fellowships to emerge.

The least reached

At its most basic level, there is a clear overlap of environmental problems with the least reached. This would easily be explored through mapping, utilising the information known about the location of the least reached with existing environmental databases. However, a few examples will suffice.

There are huge issues with desertification along the southern boundary of the Sahara, an area with a high number of least reached. Countries in this area are proposing a 'green wall' to stop the spread of the desert, a huge opportunity to plant trees—and fellowships. Coastal fishing communities of the Indian Ocean littoral are among the least reached. Projects to care for these communities and the ocean upon which they depend represent a huge opportunity for loving our neighbours. The Bajau Laut are also known as sea nomads, ranging throughout Southeast Asia, primarily Indonesia, the Philippines, and Malaysia. They are often nationless, roaming the sea fishing, sometimes in semi-permanent housing on stilts over water. They are often mistreated and are completely dependent on the sea for their livelihoods. Clearly any project to reach this group that does not take into account the state of the environment is unlikely to succeed.

Urbanites, and many Westerners in particular, have lost the ancient connections between their place and their identity. Yet it is critical to understand that, for many of the least reached, their place influences their identity. One example from a reached community comes from an amazing book written by the Anglican Archbishop of Polynesia Winston Halapua, a Tongan. He describes a contextualised theology showing how the ocean (*Moana*) influences Polynesian faith and enhances their understanding of God. He writes:

> *There are reflections on the formation of identity of the Oceanic people through their encounters with the realities of the ocean. From the time voyaging ancestors set out in their twin-hulled canoes across vast tracts of water, this identity has emerged within the depth of our people as we have engaged with one another and with our environment.*[19]

With over one hundred fifty years of missionary work in Polynesia, faithful believers are now writing about how their place impacts their identity and enhances the body of Christ. I have wept reading this book because Rev Dr Halapua so clearly and intimately knows the ocean. The ocean deeply resonates in my own heart in ways that Christian writing about land-based creation care cannot.

Increasing urbanisation may seem to mitigate against creation care as an important factor in reaching megacities. Yet there is a renewed emphasis on urban gardening, and our understanding of the wellbeing and health impact of access to green and blue spaces grows each year.[20] Mental health in urban areas is heavily impacted by access to natural places and water. These urban areas draw resources from surrounding areas, so supply chains and the state of rural areas near megacities is critical. Additionally, many urban areas are coastal, and sea-level rise is already affecting them. The natural storm buffering qualities of mangrove forests and coral reefs are increasingly being quantified by the ecosystem services they provide to coastal cities. Conservation of these natural habitats is much more effective for coastal protection than trying to repair them after the fact or putting in manmade substitutes that are usually more costly and less effective.

Principle 6

The intersection
Clearly, creation care impacts each of our three circles depicting 'the CDLR space': community development, the least reached, and emerging VCJF. What is the intersection of these sets, and how can agencies and teams integrate creation care into their work such that we can be obedient to God in this area and participate in the reconciliation of all things?

First, agencies and teams should embrace creation care. I recently received an email from a long-term worker who, through his experience with a people group in Southeast Asia, understood the need to care for the ocean—because God's ocean was suffering but also because the people they loved depended upon that diminishing resource. Their mission agency was not sympathetic, so this couple is considering starting or joining another agency to do what God has revealed to them.

Encouragingly, a number of agencies have embraced creation care as an important part of the gospel. While some may still have a 'means to an end' nuance to their understanding of creation care, it is no longer uncommon to find a mission agency with a creation care arm. Sadly, too many continue to have a dualistic, individualistic, and anthropocentric vision of the gospel that is only good news to one species and often not much use in day to day life on this beautiful planet. However, groups focused solely on creation care or community development should view their work in a more integral way that contributes to vibrant communities of Jesus followers.

Creation care—conservation—is a technical discipline and as such needs technical expertise. We should encourage young people with a concern for the environment to go into conservation as a profession. One goal within A Rocha's marine conservation programme is to train young people in an integrated faith and conservation worldview to bless the 71% of God's planet that is ocean and the billions who depend upon it. This is not an optional add-on and can also be destructive if ill-conceived plans are pursued without adequate professional preparation.

Dave Bookless points out that creation care is not just the context for mission but also 'at its broadest level, the *object* of Christian mission'. This is not to be seen as 'a context for mission, or even…an optional aspect of mission for those who specialize in it, but rather as fundamentally intertwined with God's missional purposes from creation to new creation'.[21] As is the case for 'business as mission' and medical approaches, we need to develop communities of practice that help environmental missionaries to think holistically, to integrate with community development and missions thinking such that we can see people and place transformed among the least reached, resulting in emerging, vibrant fellowships of Jesus followers.

Creation care impacts and is influenced by the other principles in the CDLR paradigm. How we think about the Kingdom of God and indeed who (or what) can enter it is clearly impacted by our beliefs about God's work in all creation. Creation care is essential in demonstrating how the 'gospel impacts the whole person and people's whole contexts' (Principle 3). We 'seek the whole city's welfare' (Principle 4.2) and believe that prayer and spiritual warfare are important parts of creation care (Principle 5). 'A truly vibrant community of Jesus followers obeys *all* that Jesus commanded' (Principle 7.1) Perhaps we should use Mark's version of the Great Commission—to preach the good news to all creation—rather than Matthew's. We need professional excellence (Principle 8) and there are huge synergies (also difficulties) with community development principles (Principle 9). Creation care also resonates with Principle 10: If we are to serve the least reached, including the least-reached places, it will take intentional efforts.

HOPE IN CHRIST
Theologian Richard Bauckham writes of proximate and ultimate hope in the face of environmental crisis.[22] Proximate hope is the immediacy of an end to the current situation, whereas ultimate hope recognises that very long-term solutions to suffering will come about as Christ puts all things aright with his coming. Creation care brings proximate hope through the work of called professionals and laity who lay down their lives to care for people and place among the least reached on our planet. We can bring proximate hope, although if things do not change, the outlook for the least reached in terms of impact from environmental crises is not good. This is all through Christ in the short- or long-term. Lawrence Ko, working in the Mongolian grasslands, expresses it this way: 'Through the Green Desert Project, they declare their faith in the future hope that God can make a way in the

wastelands, that life can flourish in dry places, that the deserts of Inner Mongolia can become green again.'[23]

As we look forward to new creation, heaven coming down to Earth as many of us pray each Sunday in our Lord's prayer, we find hope in Revelation 5:9–13 where not only all nations, tribes, and tongues worship before the throne, but all creatures above and below the water do so as well. All that was broken at the fall is ultimately fixed at the cross. Even as creation groans now, we will see the consummation of all things in that new creation. It is not clear how that looks exactly, but we know that we serve a good God, who loves all he made and that he graciously calls us to be a part of that reconciliation of all things both now and forever.

ENDNOTES

[1] Olivia Rosane, 'Humans and Big Ag Livestock Now Account for 96 Percent of Mammal Biomass', *EcoWatch* (23 May 2018), https://www.ecowatch.com/biomass-humans-animals-2571413930.html.

[2] Dave Bookless, *Planetwise* (Nottingham: IVP, 2008); Richard Bauckham, *Bible and Ecology: Rediscovering the Community of Creation* (London: Darton, Longman & Todd, 2010); Jonathan A. Moo, 'The Biblical Basis for Creation Care', in Colin Bell and Robert S. White (eds), *Creation Care and the Gospel: Reconsidering the Mission of the Church* (Peabody, MA: Hendrickson, 2016), 28–42.

[3] 'The Cape Town Commitment' (Cape Town: Lausanne Movement, 2010), https://www.lausanne.org/content/ctc/ctcommitment.

[4] Colin Bell and Robert S. White (eds), *Creation Care and the Gospel: Reconsidering the Mission of the Church* (Peabody, MA: Hendrickson, 2016).

[5] 'Creation Care Missions', accessed 11 March 2020, http://www.creationcaremissions.org/.

[6] Calvin B. DeWitt, *Earth-Wise: A Biblical Response to Environmental Issues*, 2nd ed (Grand Rapids: Faith Alive Christian Resources, 2007), 49.

[7] Meric Srokosz and Robert D. Sluka, 'Creation Care of the Other 71%', in Colin Bell and Robert S. White (eds), *Creation Care and the Gospel:*

Reconsidering the Mission of the Church(Peabody, MA: Hendrickson, 2016), 225–36.

[8] 'Battling Bushfires' (A Rocha International, 2 January 2020), https://www.arocha.org/en/news/battling-bushfires/.

[9] Andrew Newsham and Shonil Bhagwat, *Conservation and Development* (London: Routledge, 2016), 248.

[10] Dilys Roe, 'Linking Biodiversity Conservation and Poverty Alleviation: A State of Knowledge Review', *CBD Technical Series* 55 (Montreal: Secretariat of the Convention on Biological Diversity, 2010), https://www.cbd.int/doc/publications/cbd-ts-55-en.pdf.

[11] Newsham and Bhagwat, *Conservation and Development*, 2016, 328.

[12] Newsham and Bhagwat, *Conservation and Development*, 2016, 329.

[13] Christophe Béné et al., 'Resilience, Poverty and Development', *Journal of International Development* 26 no. 5 (2014): 598–623, https://doi.org/10.1002/jid.2992.

[14] Newsham and Bhagwat, *Conservation and Development*, 2016, 331.

[15] Dorothy Boorse, *Loving the Least of These* (Washington, DC: National Association of Evangelicals, 2011), https://www.nae.net/loving-the-least-of-these/.

[16] Robert D. Sluka et al., 'Christians, Biodiversity Conservation and Poverty Alleviation: A Potential Synergy?', *Biodiversity* 12.2 (2011), 1–8, https://doi.org/10.1080/14888386.2011.599780.

[17] Eric Adams, Don Allen, and Bob Fish, 'Seven Themes of Fruitfulness', *International Journal of Frontier Missiology* 26, no. 2 (2009), 75–81.

[18] Craig Sorley, 'Christ, Creation Stewardship, and Missions: How Discipleship into a Biblical Worldview on Environmental Stewardship Can Transform People and Their Land', *International Bulletin of Mission Research* 35 (2011), 137.

[19] Winston Halapua, *Waves of God's Embrace: Sacred Perspectives from the Ocean* (Norwich: Canterbury, 2008), 85.

[20] Wallace J. Nichols and Celine Cousteau, *Blue Mind: The Surprising Science That Shows How Being near, in, on, or under Water Can Make You Happier, Healthier, More Connected and Better at What You Do* (London: Back Bay Books, 2015); Deborah Cracknell, *By the Sea: The Therapeutic Benefits of Being in, on and by the Water* (London: Aster, 2019).

21 Dave Bookless, 'Context or Content? The Place of the Natural Environment in World Mission', in Cathy Ross and Colin Graham Smith (eds), *Missional Conversations: A Dialogue between Theory and Praxis in World Mission* (London: SCM Press, 2018), 6.

22 Richard Bauckham, 'Ecological Hope in Crisis', in Colin Bell and Robert S. White (eds), *Creation Care and the Gospel: Reconsidering the Mission of the Church* (Peabody, MA: Hendrickson, 2016), 47.

23 Lawrence Ko, 'Can the Desert Be Green? Asian Journeys' Green Desert Project in Inner Mongolia', in Colin Bell and Robert S. White (eds), *Creation Care and the Gospel: Reconsidering the Mission of the Church* (Peabody, MA: Hendrickson, 2016), 206–7.

PRINCIPLE 7: A VISION FOR RENEWAL AND VIBRANT COMMUNITIES OF JESUS FOLLOWERS

MARK GALPIN

> *In the early 2000s, two Christian mission organisations started work in a remote part of a country in Asia. Their work focused on community health and development and non-formal education. Team members, Christians, and non-Christians worked alongside each other and community members and over several years saw significant improvements in the health of women and children, water and sanitation, food security, literacy, and a range of other indicators. Contact was made with a church in a different region of the country and a pastor was sent to plant the first church in the area. Christian staff supported him, his family, and the fledgling fellowship in a variety of ways. Significant opposition was experienced locally by church members, and sadly, the church split within a few years over a dispute between two leaders; staff members continued to support both churches. Nearly twenty years later, there are over ten churches in this area with upwards of 200 members. Significant developmental improvements have continued in the area through the work of the government and a number of NGOs. A number of churches are also serving their wider communities in a variety of ways.*

The story above illustrates the challenges and opportunities of the intersection between community development and church planting in least-reached areas. Both mission agencies involved had restrictions placed on them by the government forbidding them from 'proselytising' activities. Both agencies' vision for this remote area included the establishment of a church by local people as a key part of the transformation process. The missions' commitment to the development of the communities they served was genuine. Community development was not the 'cover' for the real work of 'church planting', but the vision for transformation included the opportunity for people to experience freedom in Christ and join in the work of transformation and the establishment of God's Kingdom.

What do we mean by 'transformation', and how can community development contribute to this? We argue that this is only possible if it engages a vision for vibrant communities of Jesus followers (VCJF) and renewal of the whole person and community (Principle

7). Seen from this perspective, 'community transformation' blurs traditional boundaries separating church planting and community development by demonstrating the synergy and connection between these spheres of activity.

WHAT IS 'TRANSFORMATION'?

The term 'transformation' has been increasingly used in both missiology and Christian development circles over the last three decades. Wayne Bragg records the suggestion of 'transformation' as an alternative term for 'development' being made at the Wheaton Consultation on the Church in Response to Human Need in 1983.[1] In Christian development circles, the term has been popularised by Bryant Myers in his seminal work *Walking with the Poor*.[2] However, the term has also been used in wider missiological thinking as part of the movement towards a more holistic or integral praxis of mission. 'Mission as transformation' emerged as a stream of thinking, particularly from South Asia, that emphasised mission as a witness and journey within the world—the integral relation of evangelism and social action and a total commitment to the social community and building communities of change.[3] Melba Maggay's brief but influential book *Transforming Society* explored the role of the church in the process of societal transformation and approaches to this.[4] In the 'Declaration on Integral Mission' stemming from its September 2001 meeting at the Oxford Centre for Mission Studies,[5] the Micah Network played a significant role in popularising the term 'integral mission,' using it synonymously with the term 'holistic transformation'. 'Transformation' is now commonly, and perhaps at times too easily, used among Christian agencies involved in mission and community development.

The Greek word *metamorphóō*, translated as 'transformation' or 'to change into another form', is used four times in the New Testament, including the gospel references describing Jesus' transfiguration (Matt. 17:2; Mark 9:2). Considering its scant use in Scripture, the emphasis and profile that the term 'transformation' has been given within the mission and Christian development space is surprising. In Romans 12:2 Paul urges the believers, 'Do not conform to the pattern of this world, but be transformed by the renewing of your mind.' The emphasis here is on 'transformation' as an internal change in the way we perceive and behave in the world, towards a position that is radically different to the culture and society around us. Paul's use of the word in 2 Corinthians 3:18 ('we...are being transformed into his image with ever-increasing glory, which comes from the Lord, who is the Spirit') emphasises transformation as a process rather than an end point. The Holy Spirit is the agent of that process, linking transformation with the process of individual sanctification.

The understanding of transformation within Christian circles varies. Influential in this thinking has been the work of Paul Hiebert who uses the term to examine the process of worldview change at the individual level.[6] Hiebert distinguishes between 'paradigmatic' change that occurs at conversion and 'normal' worldview change that occurs through the long-term process of discipleship, emphasising the need for both. Myers, writing from a development perspective, also puts the emphasis on transformation starting at the individual level. 'The point of greatest transformational leverage is changed people,' he writes, emphasising the need for the poor to 'recover their true identity and discover the vocation God intends for them.'[7] While emphasising the need for change at the individual level and the importance of gaining a biblical perspective on their identity and purpose, this gives a rather linear and individualistic view of the transformation process. Other authors, for example Maggay, use the term transformation to emphasise structural change at the societal level.[8]

'Transformation' is a term increasingly used in secular community development circles. The emphasis here is usually on the need for wholesale structural or system level change, with little emphasis on individual change. Often secular understandings focus on an individual's values and worldview being a product of the system rather than a determinant of it. However, Bob Mitchell argues that the importance of 'inner change' is beginning to be recognised in mainstream development discourse.[9] Margaret Ledwith, a leading thinker on community development in the United Kingdom, makes the point that for community development to be transformative it must address the structural causes of poverty as the root of the problems, not just the symptoms. However, she links structural change with the need for change at the individual level, stating that:

> *The way that we understand our world shapes the way we live in our world. It is by challenging the way we see the world that we open ourselves to new worldviews, new possibilities for creating a world that is just, sustainable, and non-violent, and this new understanding in turn changes the way we live our lives.*[10]

While different authors have different emphases, understandings of transformation from secular and Christian perspectives include changes that occur from the personal through to the structural level. Transformation can therefore be defined as 'a process of positive change in the attitudes, values, and beliefs of individuals and communities leading to long-term structural change'.[11] This simple definition highlights the need for change to occur at all levels—from the worldview, value, attitudes, and practice of the individual through the community and local institutions to the higher-level structures of society—whether we talk of 'transformation' from either a secular or Christian perspective.

While there is commonality in thinking of the levels where change must occur, Christian thinking has a very different idea of who the main agents of this change are, what processes are involved, and what the outcomes or goals of transformation may be. As Christians, we acknowledge that it is not we or the community who are primary agents of change; it is God through his Holy Spirit that transforms. The process of transformation therefore involves changes both individual and corporate, spiritual and social, highlighting the need to break down unbiblical distinctions and dichotomies in our thinking and practice of mission and community development.

CHALLENGES IN BRINGING TOGETHER COMMUNITY DEVELOPMENT AND 'PROCLAMATION'

While it is easy to talk and write about the centrality of the spiritual in the process of transformation, and the importance of a vision for VCJF as part of our community work, the reality is more challenging. Much has been written on the relationship between proclamation and demonstration, or evangelism and social justice, and a diversity of positions remains.[12] While some degree of resolution has been achieved on paper, tensions remain in the practical outworking of this integration at the ground level.

Principle 7

Those focusing on community development and social justice often express concern that combining evangelism with their work communicates the implicit message that community members should profess faith if they are to continue to benefit from the social activities of the organisation. This is a valid concern and reaction against inappropriate and coercive forms of evangelism. These are often undertaken by well-intended people who seek to inappropriately balance their social and evangelistic activities amid situations of vulnerability, often resulting in more harm than good. This concern is reflected by Mitchell who warns against 'programmatic' attempts at evangelism and argues for more 'organic' approaches.[13] Much helpful work has been done in clarifying the ethical boundaries of proclamatory activity, something I explore in another section of this book.

This concern is also a reflection of ongoing suspicions toward faith-based organisations by actors within the secular aid industry, who often place explicit restrictions on any activity that could be construed as evangelistic or proselytising. Faith-based organisations that rely heavily on secular funding are understandably influenced to remain compliant with these restrictions to maintain this funding and the scale of their operations.[14]

Faith-based organisations that work within restrictive contexts also face suspicion from governments that believe their community health and development work is really a cover for proselytising activities. This is just one aspect of the well-documented shrinking of operational space afforded to NGOs and civil society in general across many parts of the world.[15] Some choose to keep their faith 'under the radar' of government attention with all the dangers this poses for themselves and others in the event of a backlash if exposed. Others emphasise the importance of integrity, transparency, and even witness in their relationship with the government. Great wisdom is needed in the leadership of these organisations as they negotiate the fine line between maintaining their faith identity and the spiritual within their work. My own observation is that often local Christian organisations and teams are much bolder than internationals in intentionally sharing their faith with those they serve, even in contexts of significant restriction and persecution, demonstrating a concern for the whole of their lives both now and into eternity.[16]

The result of these pressures is at times a position that discourages any hint of proclamatory activity, with witness being reduced simply to the quality of the work that we do and the distinctiveness of how we live. While affirming the importance of both 'being' and 'doing' aspects of bearing witness, without any 'saying' there is a danger that we become either 'signs pointing nowhere' or signs that simply point to our own good deeds and actions.[17] These can be misunderstood and fundamentally undermine the effectiveness of the work of transformation that we are involved in.

RESOLVING THE TENSIONS
One helpful distinction to avoid this dilution of our witness is to distinguish between the restrictions placed on the organisation, and those placed on individuals working for the organisation. In my own experience of working for a large, faith-based organisation focused on community health and development in a restrictive setting, our Christian staff members concluded that government restrictions placed on our organisation applied to them as individuals and that they should avoid sharing the gospel verbally with community members we worked with. In this sense, self-censorship had become more limiting than the actual social or governmental restrictions in place.

Our approach was to clarify that, while restrictions placed on our organisation meant that we would not have any programmed evangelistic activities, they as individuals not only had a basic human right to manifest their own faith (Article 18 of Universal Declaration of Human Rights) but that as Christians they had a biblical responsibility to do this. A key verse for us was: But in your hearts revere Christ as Lord. Always be prepared to give an answer to everyone who asks you to give the reason for the hope that you have. But do this with gentleness and respect (1 Pet. 3:15). We also emphasised the importance of them as individuals supporting the local church where it existed in our working areas and made this a key part of the role of our team leaders, even when it was not appropriate or possible to have a formal partnership with the local church.

Quality long-term community development work undertaken by people marked by their commitment to Christ leads to deep

Principle 7

relationships and inevitably to conversations about faith. Frequently our Christian staff, both expatriate and local, recounted stories of local people asking questions and comments such as, 'Why is it that you live in this remote area? Why do you treat us so differently to others who have worked with us?' Or even, 'You must be paid a lot of money to work here.' All these provided opportunities for explaining our motivation and inspiration and often led to deep conversations about faith and the sharing of the gospel. It is not only through the work that we do but by doing 'life' together that these opportunities arise, as the story below illustrates.

> *A local team leader of our work in a remote district was travelling to another region of the country with a non-Christian colleague. This involved a 30-minute flight through treacherous terrain. Ten minutes into the flight, the aeroplane hit a large bird, breaking the cockpit windscreen and seriously injuring the captain. The plane went into a tailspin and plummeted towards the ground. Miraculously, the co-pilot managed to regain control and land the plane safely at a local airstrip. On disembarking from the plane, all the passengers turned to our team leader and asked him why he had not screamed out in terror with the rest of the passengers as the plane spun out of control. He explained that, as a Christian, he trusted that God was in control in all situations and that God had given him peace in his heart, enabling him to pray rather than to cry out in fear.*

The power of a praying, serving presence, and the opportunities that this provides for informal verbal sharing of the gospel have been noted by other authors. Johannes Reimer proposes a cycle of service, dialogue, engagement, and sharing, emphasising the need to 'expose ourselves to questions about our faith and life' and to be bold in explaining the gospel and leading people to faith when they ask for this.[18] While the context will determine how 'bold' we can and should be, our willingness and preparedness to share (or to enable sharing by others) the gospel sensitively in any and all contexts should be a hallmark of biblical approaches to community development.

However, we also must not fall into the trap of thinking that community members becoming Christians will inevitably lead to a transformed community. Maggay makes it clear that a lack of personal transformation after conversion (due to a lack of deep discipleship) and the reality of institutional evil mean that evangelism alone does not lead to a just society and must be accompanied by 'concrete redemptive action' in all spheres of life.[19] Our vision of transformation should therefore include those who have responded to that witness and committed their lives to Christ meeting in fellowship with others as VCJF, and working towards the transformation and blessing of their own community and wider society.

THE CALL OF THE LOCAL CHURCH AND VCJF TO 'BE A BLESSING'

The identity of God as he who loves to bless is emphasised from the beginning of the biblical story. Christopher Wright in his seminal work *The Mission of God* states that Genesis as a book is 'saturated with concern for blessing'. Wright defines the biblical idea of blessing as being

> *initially and strongly connected with creation and enjoying all the good gifts that God longs for people to enjoy in his world…yet at the same time these things are to be enjoyed within the context of healthy relationships with God and with others.*[20]

He goes on to emphasise the universality of the Abrahamic promise of blessing inclusive of all nations and how this has been fulfilled by the death and resurrection of Christ: 'In Christ alone, through the gospel of his death and resurrection, stands the hope of blessing for all nations.'[21]

Roy Godwin defines blessing as 'a multiplication of God's favour resulting in prosperity, fruitfulness and…victory over enemies' leading to 'prosperity in relationships and strong community'. Godwin also emphasises that 'God's heart is to bless…and we are called to imitate him', linking the idea of blessing with the Old Testament concept of bringing *shalom*,[22] the expressed goal of transformational development.[23]

In contrast to the common use of the word transformation, the language of 'blessing' is often absent from the work of community development, perhaps because people-centred approaches to community development emphasise the importance of local people and communities bringing about change for themselves, using their own resources, whereas blessing is something that comes from 'outside'. In this, perhaps, Christian approaches to community development have been overly influenced by their secular counterpart.

Principle 7

Without undermining the important principles of 'participation' and 'empowerment', as Christians we need to reclaim the biblical concept of 'blessing' and our role of 'blessing' the communities that we are part of and serve. This is not simply blessing by what we do or changes brought about by our involvement but is something that God does. Rather than focusing our prayers on issues we face and asking for blessing on our activities and our work, we need to reclaim the idea of pronouncing God's blessing over the areas and communities in which we work.

Godwin identifies three distinctive areas that we should speak blessing over: individuals, communities, and the land. In describing the ministry of the Ffald-y-Brenin Trust and retreat centre in Wales, he illustrates these three areas with stories of individual healing and restoration, towns and communities that have prospered socially and economically, and land that has been restored ecologically and agriculturally, producing abundant harvests.[24]

The idea of God blessing the land and its inhabitants is profoundly biblical (Deut. 28:8). Shared with me by a friend serving in Egypt, the following vignette illustrates the power of praying blessing in contexts of poverty, not only over people but also over locations.

> *A missionary in Cairo walked to work every day, his route taking him past a stinking rubbish dump. For the first few months of his time there, he resented having to walk past this, but then he felt God challenging him to pronounce blessing over it. This he began to do, pronouncing God's blessing over the rubbish dump as he walked past it twice a day. Some months later he returned from a furlough break in his own country and was astounded to find that the rubbish dump had been cleared and replaced by a beautiful rose garden—an extremely rare sight in inner-city Cairo. He put this down to God answering his prayers to bless this location.*

Our community development work is an outworking of God's blessing, but the work of blessing does not end with our community work. It is taken up by those who have put their faith in Jesus and committed to follow in his footsteps, obeying all he has commanded them to do. The VCJF that emerge as part of our vision of transformation should therefore take up the responsibility as God's people to be distinctive in how they live their lives as agents of blessing and bringers of *shalom* through the power of the Holy Spirit.

The establishment of VCJF is therefore not only a sign of true transformation but is also critical to ensuring the process of transformation is sustained beyond our community engagement. While a holistic ministry should lead to a holistic perspective and ministry for those who are the fruit of that ministry, this is not always the case. Community engagement and transformation needs to be pro-actively and deliberately included in the processes of discipleship and leadership training to ensure this.

CONCLUSION
'Transformation' involves changes ranging from the individual through to the community, institutional, and structural levels of society. Spiritual change involving both conversion and deep discipleship is central to any real process of transformation. This can only happen by the power of the Holy Spirit. This kind of change is an act of God's mercy and grace and may occur even if we are somewhat haphazard or do not really know what we are doing. But while we recognise the impact of context on how we work, and the importance of adapting sensitively to that context, the emergence of vibrant communities of Jesus followers should nevertheless be central to our prayers and vision for community transformation. While contextual challenges and the danger of implicit coercive messages often make the inclusion of formal programmatic approaches to evangelism with our community development unwise, the equipping of our staff and partners to 'give a reason for the hope that is within them...with gentleness and respect' (1 Pet. 3:15) is a critical component of transformational community development in least-reached settings.

Incorporating the profoundly biblical concept of 'blessing' into both our community development work and into the discipleship and training of our staff and leaders of the emerging churches is important in ensuring that we and they are faithful to the call to 'be a blessing' and to sustain the process of transformation.

ENDNOTES

[1] Wayne G. Bragg, 'From Development to Transformation', in Vinay Samuel and Chris Sugden (eds), *The Church in Response to Human Need* (Oxford: Regnum, 1987), 38.

[2] Bryant L. Myers, *Walking with the Poor: Principles and Practices of Transformational Development*, Rev. ed. (Maryknoll: Orbis, 2011).

[3] Vinay Samuel, 'Mission as Transformation', in Vinay Samuel and Chris Sugden (eds), *Mission as Transformation: A Theology of the Whole Gospel* (Oxford: Regnum, 1999), 227–35.

[4] Melba Padilla Maggay, *Transforming Society* (Quezon City, Philippines: Institute for Studies in Asian Church and Culture, 1996); Melba Padilla Maggay, *Transforming Society* (Eugene: Wipf & Stock, 2011).

[5] Micah Network, 'Micah Network Declaration on Integral Mission' (27 September 2001), https://www.micahnetwork.org/sites/default/files/doc/page/mn_integral_mission_declaration_en.pdf.

[6] Paul G. Hiebert, *Transforming Worldviews: An Anthropological Understanding of How People Change* (Grand Rapids: Baker Academic, 2008).

[7] Myers, *Walking with the Poor*, 2011, 178–79.

[8] Maggay, *Transforming Society*, 1996.

[9] Bob Mitchell, *Faith-Based Development: How Christian Organizations Can Make a Difference* (Maryknoll: Orbis, 2017), 91.

[10] Margaret Ledwith, *Community Development: A Critical Approach*, 2nd ed (Bristol: Policy Press, 2011), 10.

[11] I am indebted to the United Mission to Nepal (UMN) for this working definition of transformation.

[12] See, for example, Tim Chester, *Is Everything Mission?* (Nottingham: Keswick Ministries, 2019); John R. W. Stott and Christopher J. H. Wright, *Christian Mission in the Modern World*, Updated ed. (Downers Grove: InterVarsity, 2015).

[13] Mitchell, *Faith-Based Development*, 2017, 95.

[14] Mitchell, *Faith-Based Development*, 2017, 162.

[15] Adele Poskitt, 'Changes in the International Development Landscape: Social Sector Organizations from the Emerging Powers', in S. Aqeel Tirmizi and John D. Vogelsang (eds), *Leading and Managing in the Social Sector*, Management for Professionals (Cham, Switzerland: Springer, 2016), 91–108.

[16] The witness of those from the local community can be much more fruitful than that of foreigners, particularly in contexts where Christianity is seen as a foreign religion, though this does not preclude the need for foreign workers also to 'be prepared to give an answer to everyone who asks you to give the reason for the hope that you have' (1 Pet. 3:15).

[17] Tim Chester, *Good News to the Poor: Sharing the Gospel through Social Involvement* (Leicester: Inter-Varsity Press, 2004).

[18] Johannes Reimer, *Missio Politica: The Mission of Church and Politics* (Carlisle: Langham, 2017), 89.

[19] Maggay, *Transforming Society*, 1996, 17.

[20] Christopher J. H. Wright, *The Mission of God: Unlocking the Bible's Grand Narrative* (Downers Grove: IVP Academic, 2006), 221.

[21] Wright, *The Mission of God*, 2006, 221.

[22] Roy Godwin, *The Way of Blessing: Stepping into the Mission and Presence of God* (Colorado Springs: David C Cook, 2016), 132–33.

[23] Myers, *Walking with the Poor*, 2011, 177–83.

[24] Godwin, *The Way of Blessing*, 2016.

PRINCIPLE 8:
COMMUNITY DEVELOPMENT WORKERS ARE COMMITTED TO PROFESSIONAL EXCELLENCE

SCOTT BRESLIN

A commitment to professional excellence is a devotion to consistently satisfy or surpass the criteria of key stakeholders. In this discussion on professional excellence, I argue that the criteria by which faith-based community development practitioners are judged stems from their accountability to seven stakeholders. These include:
1. Affected people (the client or participant)
2. Host government (both local and national)
3. Donors
4. International development sector (the profession itself)
5. The development workers' organisation
6. The development worker (self-conscientiousness)
7. God

For international development practitioners, the criteria for achieving professional excellence is complicated because they are accountable to seven different bosses. While this is ordinarily to be avoided, in the international aid sector it is the norm. It requires development workers to give priority to the criteria of the stakeholder(s) to whom the worker has the greatest moral obligation—in most cases, the affected people. While it is true that all people are ultimately accountable to God, it is also true that God, actively involved in all people, consistently uses human organisations, faith-based or not, to accomplish his purposes. However, those of us in the Christian tradition recognise that God has specifically aligned himself with the causes of the suffering and marginalised. Therefore, I will try to show that the criteria of affected people are normally consistent with the priorities of God and not easily distinguishable from one another.

In this chapter, I devote most of the discussion to the notion that God is the key stakeholder in community development work, especially for faith-based NGOs. However, Christians should not see God as one among seven stakeholders but rather as the one stakeholder who is actively working in and through all stakeholders to accomplish his purposes, including defending the suffering and vulnerable. Based on a Christian perspective, I make several suggestions regarding the criteria God uses for judging excellence. First, I will briefly describe the other six stakeholders using real-life examples to highlight the complexities of navigating conflicting expectations.

1. THE AFFECTED PEOPLE OR COMMUNITY
People and communities affected by suffering and marginalisation are the most important stakeholders in humanitarian and development work but frequently are the least consulted. In the 1980s and 1990s, Michael Edwards was one of many voices calling for reforms in both international development studies and expert-centric development practices. He asserts that when training institutes promote a technocratic, project-oriented, 'we know better' approach to professional practice, it is doomed to irrelevancy and likely to make bad situations worse.

> *What is required is a* people's science *which uses local knowledge to explore local solutions to local problems. Such a* science *differs radically in approach from the traditional one, which ignores indigenous knowledge or relegates it to a subordinate position.*[1]

Today, thanks to people like Edwards, within the international aid sector professionalism has moved away from 'we know better' to concepts that are more participatory and have the people affected at the centre. A commitment to professional excellence keeps affected people at the centre of project work. Here is a testimony from my doctoral research interview of a colleague named Peter who worked in Darfur. His strong personal relationship with the elders of recently displaced villages in Darfur allowed him to advocate on their behalf to UN agencies and keep them, rather than political agendas, at the centre.

> *We started working in IDP camps since all the villages in one of our project areas were displaced because of bombing by the [Sudan] government. So, we followed them to the IDP camp and started to set up a clinic there working with them. I was pushing hard because no services were being provided. It*

Principle 8

didn't fit the political rhetoric of 'It's time to return people from IDP camps' *and nobody was doing anything about all these displaced people. But* they were my friends. *These were people* we worked with for years and years. *We helped them set up a pretty good life in their villages and now they were sitting under a tree with nothing because the government bombed their villages. So, when I took OCHA (United Nations Office for the Coordination of Humanitarian Affairs) and WHO (World Health Organization) and other people out there they said it looked more like a family reunion when we arrived than normal NGO work. They were somehow surprised that we had established trusted relationships with the people. We were not just doing work but* there were also relationships.[2]

2. THE HOST GOVERNMENT

International community development work is always performed at the invitation of or with the permission of host governments, both national and local. That invitation/permission comes with conditions and criteria. Community development workers are accountable to their host government. Sometimes it is not a problem, but quite frequently host governments have criteria and expectations that are incompatible with other stakeholders' priorities. Frequently, the host government's neglect, corruption, and policies are primary causes of the human suffering that the aid worker is there to help alleviate. To achieve professional excellence, community development workers need to carefully consider the spoken and unspoken expectations of the host government.

During my interview with Peter, I commented that his relationship with the government seemed somewhat tenuous. I suggested that sometimes the Sudanese government were good guys, and sometimes they were bad guys. He responded:

No, they are usually the bad guys. They have their own very strong agenda. We try to keep them happy enough to not kick us out. If we were to just do what they want us to do we would never be in the area that had the biggest health needs. We would just be in the areas that the government controls. They now use humanitarian aid as a weapon against the people.

In Peter's experience, the host government of Sudan was the chief villain of the crisis in Darfur. I interviewed other development workers who worked in Central Asia or the Middle East and had similar but less extreme feelings that their presence was tolerated but not wanted; government officials demanded bribes, blocked visa applications, or pursued agendas that, in development workers' opinions, were not in the best interest of the crisis-affected people. Instead of cooperation, there is frequently underlying tension between development workers and their host governments. In such circumstances, what does a commitment to professional excellence look like?

There are times when government criteria and their officials are aligned with the other stakeholders. When this happens, it is a beautiful thing to behold. Rosemary Hack describes such a setting in the closing sections of Chapter 10.

3. THE DONORS
Donors have their own criteria and priorities regarding how funds are spent. It is natural for both government and private donors to invest their money according to their own goals and priorities. Nilima Gulrajani and Rachael Calleja point out:

> There is little doubt that foreign aid enables the pursuit, promotion and defence of the national interests of the donor nation and has done for some time. No country would provide aid if it did not serve, or was at least benign to, its own concerns and priorities. At the same time, donors are clearly capable of generosity towards and solidarity with international causes and crises—perhaps most visible in the case of natural disasters and humanitarian assistance.[3]

Community development workers are accountable to their donors. Professional excellence requires the donors' criteria to be consistent with that of the other six stakeholders. When donors embrace the Core Humanitarian Standard on Quality and Accountability (see number 4) the risk of the donors' agenda being in conflict with other stakeholders' agendas is greatly reduced.

Faith-based community development workers potentially have additional donor conflict dilemmas unique to them. There are many donors who insist that Christian development workers do not engage in 'proselytisation' while associated with projects they are funding while some donors have expectations that evangelism does take place. These are interesting but not new dilemmas. I have seen both secular and Islamic media justify the murder of Christian aid workers with comments such as, 'They must have been proselytising.' I have also witnessed well-intended but misguided

Principle 8

Christians who thought humanitarian aid could be used as a cover for evangelism. I have included a short discussion on this below. In any case, faith-based community development workers must carefully consider how the expectations of donors align with the criteria of the other stakeholders.

4. THE INTERNATIONAL DEVELOPMENT SECTOR (I.E. THE PROFESSION ITSELF)

Over the past thirty years, international aid in general, and humanitarian aid specifically, has experienced different initiatives to professionalise. According to Peter Walker and Catherine Russ, in order to professionalise humanitarian aid work, key stakeholders will need to:
   a. Agree on codes of conduct and standards of practice in the profession
   b. Agree on the qualifications for credentialing/licensing practitioners
   c. Form a professional organisation that accredits and monitors training providers, credentials/licences, and professionals.[4]

This has proven to be difficult because the globalised nature of international aid, the diversity of the actors, and the contexts make the process particularly complex. There is now a strong consensus in the international aid sector that the traditional notion of 'we know better than you' must be replaced by a professionalism that embraces participation, facilitation, cooperation, and contextual thinking. As Robert Chambers observes,

> *The new participatory professionalism embraces self-critical reflection and learning, unlearning and unceasing personal and professional change.*[5]

The CHS Alliance has been instrumental in helping humanitarian and development aid communities articulate a general consensus regarding criteria for excellence and good practice. The Core Humanitarian Standard (CHS),[6] summarised in the accompanying table, has become the de facto criteria for best practice. This set of nine criteria for humanitarian and development actors is designed to measure the quality and effectiveness of aid work. I see no obvious conflict between these nine principles articulated in the CHS and what Jesus and his disciples taught in the New Testament; if others do see a conflict, I would love to discuss it. In my opinion, these principles provide a beautiful example of the common ground that can be shared between Christians and non-Christians in the humanitarian and development aid space.

Because it is the most universally accepted set of professional standards and principles for international humanitarian and development workers, it plays a central role in harmonising project criteria among all stakeholders. A commitment to professional excellence in community development will, whenever possible, incorporate the criteria of the CHS.

Summary of the Core Humanitarian Standard
on Quality and Accountability

Communities and people affected by crisis…

1. receive assistance appropriate and relevant to their needs.
2. have access to the humanitarian assistance they need at the right time.
3. are not negatively affected and are more prepared, resilient, and less at-risk as a result of humanitarian action.
4. know their rights and entitlements, have access to information, and participate in decisions that affect them.
5. have access to safe and responsive mechanisms to handle complaints.
6. receive coordinated, complementary assistance.
7. can expect delivery of improved assistance as organisations learn from experience and reflection.
8. receive the assistance they require from competent and well-managed staff and volunteers.
9. can expect that the organisations assisting them are managing resources effectively, efficiently, and ethically.

---

5. THE WORKER'S ORGANISATION

Community development workers are accountable to their organisation's own set of criteria and policies by which they internally judge the quality of their staff's work. However, some implementing

Principle 8

organisations' decision-making systems and organisational structures are not easily conducive to professional excellence on the ground. For example, field workers of organisations that use centralised strategic decision-making will struggle to fulfil the expectations of the CHS. Unless field staff are delegated authority to make decisions on behalf of the organisation, it is nearly impossible to have sufficient programme flexibility and contextual dexterity to enable the people affected by a crisis to participate in decisions affecting them. Implementing organisations need to carefully align their operating principles so they are not contradictory or inconsistent with the CHS.

6. THE WORKER (SELF-CONSCIENTIOUSNESS)

Development practitioners are themselves stakeholders—autonomous actors with their own motivations, strengths, insecurities, and personalities. They are accountable to act in a manner consistent with their conscience and other internal monitors.

A growing sense of self-awareness is critical for professional excellence. Our motivations are complex and often unknowable, frequently tainted by our insecurities, misinformation, selfishness, and pride. What looks from the outside as noble and excellent can be driven by dark motivations. I frequently find myself praying:

> *Search me, God, and know my heart; test me and know my anxious thoughts. See if there is any offensive way in me, and lead me in the way everlasting. (Psa. 139:23–24)*

When we discover unflattering motivations within ourselves, it is best to turn away from them as soon as possible. While motivations are often unknowable, over time they normally reveal themselves in our attitudes and actions. Each individual worker has their own personal perceptions for judging excellence.

Our conscience is an important but not flawless internal monitor that provides criteria for deciding right and wrong and what is well done or poorly done. A commitment to professional excellence requires the development professional to have a growing sense of self-awareness and a life-long commitment to self-development.

7. GOD

Faith-based NGOs consider God as the key stakeholder among all the actors in international aid. In the Christian tradition, God is seen as the defender and advocate of the marginalised and suffering. For example:

> *Whoever oppresses the poor shows contempt for their Maker, but whoever is kind to the needy honours God. (Prov. 14:31)*
>
> *Speak up for those who cannot speak for themselves, for the rights of all who are destitute. Speak up and judge fairly; defend the rights of the poor and needy. (Prov. 31:8–9)*
>
> *Religion that God our Father accepts as pure and faultless is this: to look after orphans and widows in their distress and to keep oneself from being polluted by the world. (Jas. 1:27)*

God is the stakeholder to whom all other stakeholders must give account. In the New Testament, God is actively organising and working in both Christian and non-Christians to help protect and look after the poor and vulnerable. There are also instructions in the New Testament compatible with a 'commitment to professional excellence'. These are explored below.

JESUS AND THE NOTION OF PROFESSIONAL EXCELLENCE

There are teachings in the New Testament that support the idea that excellence at work should be the ambition of everyone who follows Jesus. Jesus makes this point in the Sermon on the Mount, commanding his followers:

> *In the same way, let your light shine before others, that they may see your good deeds and glorify your Father in heaven. (Matt. 5:16)*

Jesus tells his disciples that their 'good deeds' should be done in such a way that they bring glory to God. Let's take a closer look at what Jesus means by good deeds.

The Greek words *kalos* and *ergon* (here and below I use their singular forms) are rightly translated in English as 'good deeds'. The issue, however, is that the phrase 'good works' or 'good deeds' evokes a much narrower meaning to English readers than they would have for readers of ancient Greek.

What normally comes to mind for an English speaker is an act of kindness, like buying a meal for a beggar on the street or helping elderly people cross a busy street. These are 'good works', but the meaning in Greek is much broader and comprehensive. Reviewing the standard Greek lexicons points to a broader range of meanings of these words, including concepts such as:

Kalos: *noble, praiseworthy, honourable, excellent, or beautiful.*

Ergon: *deeds, employment, actions, occupation, or anything accomplished by hand, art, industry, or mind.*

The meaning behind the Greek phrase is not limited to good deeds such as volunteering at a homeless shelter; it refers to any work, employment, action, or industry that is good, noble, excellent, beautiful, or praiseworthy. Jesus expects his followers to aim for professional excellence because he commands them to do *kalos* (excellent) *ergon* (works).

Let's look at it from several other angles. The apostle Paul, writing to followers of Jesus in the city of Ephesus, said:

For we are God's handiwork, created in Christ Jesus to do good works, which God prepared in advance for us to do. (Eph. 2:10)

Perhaps God has prepared in advance beggars who need meals and elderly people who need help crossing busy streets. But the context here demands a broader understanding of 'good works'. Paul teaches that followers of Jesus were created in Christ Jesus to do *kalos ergon*—'good works'—similar to Jesus' exhortation in Matthew 5:16. Paul is providing an answer to one of the deepest questions of life: Why do I exist? Why has God made me? The answer, according to Paul, is to do excellent works that God has prepared for us to do using the gifts and opportunities he has given us.

GOD ORCHESTRATES THE ACTIVITIES OF ALL STAKEHOLDERS (CHRISTIAN AND NON-CHRISTIAN) TO MEET THE NEEDS OF PEOPLE

According to the New Testament, any 'good' work that serves others can bring praise to God, not only that which alleviates poverty and suffering. Consider the following verse in the Lord's prayer. Here Jesus teaches his disciples to ask their Father in heaven to '[g]ive us today our daily bread' (Matt. 6:11).

Practically all followers of Jesus expect God to answer this prayer, but virtually none expect a loaf of bread to supernaturally appear. Undoubtedly, God could do so if he wanted, but that is not how God normally answers prayer for bread and other needs; he uses other humans as his agents of provision. In the case of bread, he uses farmers, millers, bakers, grocery store workers, and others in the supply chain. When supply chains function well, they do not appear to be particularly miraculous processes, but God seems to delight in allowing people (including non-Christians) to participate with him (knowingly or unknowingly) in answering the prayers of others. Thus, God gives dignity and meaning to everyone in the supply chain working for the common good. This is another reason to strive for excellence at work: God uses your good works to answer others' prayers.

The same is true with the collection of actors involved in humanitarian and development aid. God normally orchestrates the activities of human agents, human supply chains, and a variety of human stakeholders to protect and care for the suffering and vulnerable. However, human greed, corruption, and false assumptions frequently disrupt human supply chains meant to meet the needs of others.

Martin Luther suggested that whether a person has a vocation as a prince or a labourer, what makes an action 'good' is that it is done to serve others. He wrote:

> *The prince should think: Christ has served me and made everything to follow him; therefore, I should also serve my neighbor, protect him and everything that belongs to him. That is why God has given me this office, and I have it that I might serve him. That would be a good prince and ruler. When a prince sees his neighbor oppressed, he should think: That concerns me! I must protect and shield my neighbor...The same is true for shoemaker, tailor, scribe, or reader. If he is a Christian tailor, he will say: I make these clothes because God has bidden me do so, so that I can earn a living, so that I can help and serve my neighbor. When a Christian does not serve the other, God is not present; that is not Christian living.*[7]

In Luther's view, being a politician, shoemaker, or tailor was no less of a calling than being a monk. Undoubtedly, if community development practitioners had existed in Martin Luther's day, he would have urged them to consider their work a calling from God and to do it with excellence as both a means to earn a living and to serve.

Principle 8

The apostle Paul instructed the followers of Jesus, particularly those who were slaves:

> *Whatever you do, work at it with all your heart, as working for the Lord, not for human masters (Col. 3:23)*
>
> *Serve wholeheartedly, as if you were serving the Lord, not people, because you know that the Lord will reward each one for whatever good they do, whether they are slave or free. (Eph. 6:7–8)*

Paul understands that practically any work, when done wholeheartedly for the Lord and not just to please men, is an act of worship that pleases God. Even while doing unpleasant or menial work, followers of Jesus are instructed to work wholeheartedly unto God.

REPRESENTING JESUS IN THE WORKPLACE

In my three decades of working in faith-based aid organisations and for-profit multinational corporations, I always understood it was my privilege to represent Jesus in my work. It is hard to read the New Testament and not get the impression that God has given followers of Jesus the responsibility to represent him in their work, communities, and families. Since the New Testament never uses the word proselytisation, I do not think it is something for Christians to concern themselves with. Jesus did tell his followers to disciple others and has given Christians responsibility for the message of reconciliation between God and mankind. As such, Christians are told they are Christ's ambassadors, representing Jesus wherever they are. The apostle Paul said it like this:

> *All this is from God, who reconciled us to himself through Christ and gave us the ministry of reconciliation: that God was reconciling the world to himself in Christ, not counting people's sins against them. And he has committed to us the message of reconciliation. We are therefore Christ's ambassadors, as though God were making his appeal through us. We implore you on Christ's behalf: Be reconciled to God. (2 Cor. 5:18–20)*

Not only are followers of Jesus ambassadors; the apostle Peter calls them a nation of priests:

But you are a chosen people, a royal priesthood, a holy nation, God's special possession, that you may declare the praises of him who called you out of darkness into his wonderful light. (1 Pet. 2:9)

Like ambassadors, priests have been given authority to represent God to people and people to God. If you are a Christian, you have a holy obligation to represent Jesus wherever you are. Representation is not proselytisation, but as representatives of Jesus, we are duty bound to invite people to hear God's message of reconciliation.

SUMMARY
Faith-based community development practitioners have seven masters. A commitment to professional excellence requires the practitioner to be mindful of the expectations of all seven stakeholders and to do what they can to meet or exceed their expectations.

The Core Humanitarian Standard on Quality and Accountability provides a set of criteria and principles that host governments, donors, implementing organisations, and practitioners should embrace, thereby significantly increasing the possibility that the expectations and criteria by which project work is judged are aligned and consistent among the stakeholders. There is no obvious clash between the CHS and the values and expectations of God as understood from the Christian tradition.

For faith-based community development practitioners within the Christian tradition, God, who is the protector and advocate of the poor, is the key stakeholder. To the degree that Christians can understand God's values and expectations, these should be factored into the faith-based organisation's approach to community development. At minimum, these include a commitment to:
1. Do excellent quality work that benefits others. (Matt. 5:16)
2. Be wholehearted, working for God and not just ourselves or others. (Col. 3:23)
3. Acknowledge that work (even for non-Christians) is a means to participate with God to meet the needs of others. (Matt. 6:11)
4. Represent Jesus in the workplace as his ambassador and priest with your words, actions, and attitudes. (2 Cor. 5:18–20)

ENDNOTES

[1] Michael Edwards, 'The Irrelevance of Development Studies', *Third World Quarterly* 11, no. 1 (January 1989), 120.

[2] Here and in the following section, I draw on my 'Exploring the Professional Journeys of Exemplary Expatriate Field Leaders in the International Aid Sector' (DEd dissertation, University of Edinburgh, 2014).

[3] Nilima Gulrajani and Rachael Calleja, 'Understanding Donor Motivations: Developing the Principled Aid Index' (Working paper, Overseas Development Institute, March 2019), https://www.odi.org/sites/odi.org.uk/files/resource-documents/12633.pdf. Sources cited by Gulrajani and Calleja are available in the online document.

[4] Peter Walker and Catherine Russ, 'Professionalising the Humanitarian Sector' (London: ELHRA, 2010), accessed 14 February 2020, https://www.elrha.org/wp-content/uploads/2015/01/Professionalising_the_humanitarian_sector.pdf.

[5] Robert Chambers, 'Reflections and Directions: A Personal Note', *PLA*, Critical reflections, future directions, 50 (October 2004), 29.

[6] 'Core Humanitarian Standard on Quality and Accountability' (CHS Alliance, 2014), https://corehumanitarianstandard.org/the-standard/language-versions. The document is available in 27 languages.

[7] Martin Luther, 'Sermon in the Castle Church at Weimar (25 October 1522)', *D. Martin Luthers Werke: Kritische Gesamtausgabe* vol. 10/3 (trans. F.J.G., Weimar: Herman Böhlaus Nachfolger, 1966), 382.

CORRUPTION, COMMUNITY DEVELOPMENT, AND THE LEAST REACHED

Martin Allaby

WHAT IS CORRUPTION?
A colleague recently spent a year reading through the Bible twice, noting the passages that are relevant to corruption. These passages appear in a wide range of the books in the Bible but are found most frequently in Proverbs and the Prophets, followed by the New Testament, the five books of the Law and the Psalms. He concluded that the Bible passages that talk about corruption fall into five main categories:
- Bribery. For example, Micah 7:3 (NLT): 'Officials and judges alike demand bribes. The people with influence get what they want, and together they scheme to twist justice.'
- Denial of justice, particularly in relation to rulings in court. For example, Isaiah 10:1–3 (NLT): 'What sorrow awaits the unjust judges and those who issue unfair laws. They deprive the poor of justice and deny the rights of the needy among my people. They prey on widows and take advantage of orphans.'
- Oppression, including arbitrary behaviour outside the law. For example, Ezekiel 45:9 (NLT): 'For this is what the Sovereign Lord says: Enough, you princes of Israel! Stop your violence and oppression and do what is just and right. Quit robbing and cheating my people out of their land. Stop expelling them from their homes, says the Sovereign Lord.'
- Gaining wealth by unjust means. For example, 1 Corinthians 6:9–10 (NLT): 'Don't you realise that those who do wrong will not inherit the Kingdom of God? Don't fool yourselves. Those who…are thieves, or greedy people…or who cheat people…none of these will inherit the Kingdom of God.'
- Dishonesty. For example, Zechariah 8:16–17 (NLT): 'But this is what you must do: Tell the truth to each other. Render verdicts in your courts that are just and that lead to peace. Don't

scheme against each other. Stop your love of telling lies that you swear are the truth. I hate all these things, says the Lord.'

Most of these five categories deal with opportunities available mainly to elites: judges who can deny justice in court; rulers who have the power to oppress others; and people who have become rich by unjust means. The Bible's condemnation of bribery is targeted at elites who use either their wealth to offer bribes or their official position to demand them, rather than the poor who are forced by corrupt officials to pay bribes. Indeed, the latter kind of 'bribery' is usually a response to extortion, rather than initiation of a corrupt transaction. The Bible's emphasis on powerful elites as the main perpetrators of corruption is reflected in Transparency International's words: 'the abuse of entrusted power for private gain',[1] the most widely used secular definition of corruption.

As for the effects of corruption, the World Bank has summarised succinctly the main ways in which it promotes poverty and undermines societies and nations:

> *Corruption has a disproportionate impact on the poor and most vulnerable, increasing costs and reducing access to services, including health, education and justice...Corruption erodes trust in government and undermines the social contract. This is cause for concern across the globe, but particularly in contexts of fragility and violence, as corruption fuels and perpetuates the inequalities and discontent that lead to fragility, violent extremism, and conflict. Corruption impedes investment, with consequent effects on growth and jobs. Countries capable of confronting corruption use their human and financial resources more efficiently, attract more investment, and grow more rapidly.*[2]

WHY IS CORRUPTION SO WIDESPREAD?

It is a sad fact that entrusted power is abused for private gain far more often than it is used for public service. Why is corruption so widespread, and so difficult to bring under control?

A few years ago, the eminent economic historian Douglass North proposed an answer along the following lines: people accept being exploited by their leaders because they would be even worse off under the alternative of anarchy, particularly from the risk of uncontrolled violence.[3] Although this was presented as a novel theory, it has some similarities with the account in 1 Samuel 8 of the Israelites' motivation for having a king and God's warnings about the consequences. God warns them (1 Sam. 8:11–17) that any king will commandeer their sons and daughters, confiscate their land, tax them, take their servants and their animals for his personal use, and ultimately they will all become slaves of the king. 'When that day comes, you will cry out for relief from the king you have chosen, but the Lord will not answer you in that day.' God's warning goes unheeded by the Israelites, because their overriding concern is physical security (1 Sam. 8:19–20): 'We want…a king to lead us and to go out before us and fight our battles.'

HOW HAVE CHRISTIANS HELPED TO CONTROL CORRUPTION?

Control of corruption depends on good governance, in which the legislature, the executive, and the judiciary—the three main institutions of the state—operate as they should. But if the individuals who occupy positions of power in those institutions are corrupt, how can the institutions be reformed? Christian faith, particularly Protestant faith, has sometimes played a significant role in motivating individuals to improve the healthy functioning of all three main institutions of the state.

Regarding the rule of law, theistic religions including Christianity spread the concept that right and wrong are determined ultimately by a heavenly authority and not merely by whichever human authority holds power. Secular historians have argued, for example, that this underlies the generally stronger rule of law in culturally Christian countries than in China, which has never had a majority theistic religion.[4]

As for the role of the executive, Protestant faith has motivated rulers and other power brokers in Europe and the USA to control corruption. For example, in the words of eminent political scientist Francis Fukuyama:

> *In each of these countries, individual leaders of reform movements were motivated by personal religiosity…From well before the English Civil War, Puritanism was an important driver of reform in England, and it continued to shape the behaviour of the new middle classes in the nineteenth century. This was true as well of the upper-crust Progressive Era reformers in late-nineteenth century America, who did not think merely that political bosses and patronage politics got in the way of making money. They were morally outraged that public offices were being perverted for private ends.[5]*

Turning to the role of the legislature, Protestant missionaries have played a more important role than anyone else in the global spread of democracy, which in turn helps to create and maintain a healthy legislature. Motivated by a desire for local converts to read the Bible in their mother tongue, Protestant missionaries catalysed mass education and mass printing, leaving behind a legacy of better educated populations with wider access to local newspapers. Since abuses by colonial rulers and businessmen undermined conversions, the missionaries used their political connections back home to challenge and moderate those abuses. The consequence is a clear correlation between the density of Protestant missionaries a century ago and the strength of democracy today.[6]

WHAT CAN THE CHURCH DO ABOUT CORRUPTION AFFECTING LEAST-REACHED COMMUNITIES?

The preceding examples provide encouragement for Christians who want to help control corruption, but they all concern contexts in which Christians held a degree of power. What about situations where the church is a tiny, perhaps persecuted, minority or where possibly none at all from the local community are followers of Jesus? With the focus of this book in mind, what can be the contribution of Christians who are engaged in community development in such settings?

Strive always to keep your conscience clear

Personal and organisational integrity can allow the body of Christ to present a healthy alternative to prevailing norms such as nepotism, favouritism, tax avoidance, and accepting bribes. However, all Christians have been socialised into the norms of the culture in which they grew up. Corruption is very widespread so, unless the Bible's teaching about integrity and corruption is carefully taught and systematically applied, the emerging community of Jesus followers may lack the distinctiveness that God seeks.

Is it always wrong to pay a bribe? This is a controversial topic. I suggest that careful assessment of the power balance between the parties involved, and their gains and losses from the transaction, can help to clarify the ethics involved. For example, a parent who is forced by a hospital worker to give an illegal payment to get essential treatment for their sick child should be seen as a victim of extortion, not a corrupt person; in my view, they should be reassured that their conscience is clear. Refusing to pay a bribe is often costly to the person who takes that stand, and it is important for expatriate workers to remember that the cost may be easier for them to bear than for local followers of Jesus.

Pray for and, if possible, encourage non-Christian reformers
Control of corruption in any country generally depends more on its reform-minded citizens, whatever their faith, than on anything that expatriates can do. One of my most rewarding experiences as a missionary was sitting alongside a doctor—a follower of another faith—who led the Health Sector Reform Unit in the Ministry of Health in his country. As we worked together on an evaluation of their annual plan, he described his loneliness and discouragement as one of a tiny minority of staff who actually wanted the government health system to improve, rather than using his position as an opportunity to steal from government coffers. At the end he remarked that, although progress was really slow and difficult, he could see that there had been some changes for the better and that it was worth persevering.

Be open to occasional opportunities to challenge the abuse of power
The Bible's prophetic challenges against corruption are concentrated in the Old Testament rather than the New, reflecting the religious allegiances of the rulers during those different periods. Most of the rulers of Old Testament Israel claimed at least some allegiance to Yahweh, and the prophets were correspondingly blunt in their denouncement of failures to reflect that in their leadership. The Roman rulers in the first century made no such claims, and both Jesus and the early Christians were correspondingly circumspect in any criticisms they made of Roman abuses of power. Nor were they entirely silent.

When Jesus said, 'Give back to Caesar what is Caesar's, and to God what is God's' (Luke 20:25), it is likely that the coin he was looking at carried this blasphemous inscription: 'Caesar Augustus Tiberius, son of the Divine Augustus'. Martin Luther interpreted Jesus' words in line with his doctrine of the 'two kingdoms', in which the Kingdom of God deals with that which is spiritual and inward, while the worldly kingdom has authority over that which is bodily and outward. But a contemporary 'kingdom' theology provides a very different interpretation. In the first half of his answer, Jesus is saying, 'That coin obviously bears the image of the emperor and his blasphemous claims, so give it back to him.' In the second half of his answer, Jesus is posing the question, 'What exactly are the things that are God's?' His Jewish listeners would recall that they belong to God and might think Jesus is pointing out that Caesar actually has no real claim on them.

Moving on to the early church, Paul used his status as a Roman citizen to challenge the misuse of power that saw him wrongfully arrested, beaten, and imprisoned without trial (Acts 16:22–24). When the magistrates realised their mistake, Paul did not go quietly but instead embarrassed them publicly by insisting they come to the prison in person to escort him and Silas out.

Remember how the story ends
Whenever I feel discouraged by the enormous challenge of fighting corruption, I turn to Revelation 21:23–27 to remind myself of how the story ends. It paints a wonderful picture of the destiny of the world as it describes rulers and nations living in right relationship with God and acting with integrity:

> *...the glory of God gives the city light, and the Lamb is its lamp. The nations will walk by its light, and the kings of the earth will bring their splendour into it...The glory and honour of the nations will be brought into it. Nothing impure will enter it, nor will anyone who does what is shameful or deceitful, but only those whose names are written in the Lamb's book of life.*

As Archbishop Tutu reminded people while holding up his Bible during the years of apartheid in South Africa, 'I have read this book to the end, and we win!'

ENDNOTES

[1] Transparency International, 'What Is Corruption?', accessed 12 March 2020, https://www.transparency.org/what-is-corruption.
[2] World Bank, 'Combating Corruption', accessed 12 March 2020, https://www.worldbank.org/en/topic/governance/brief/anti-corruption.

[3] Douglass C. North, John Joseph Wallis, and Barry R. Weingast, *Violence and Social Orders: A Conceptual Framework for Interpreting Recorded Human History* (Cambridge: Cambridge University Press, 2009), https://www.cambridge.org/core/product/identifier/9780511575839/type/book.

[4] See, for example, Francis Fukuyama, *The Origins of Political Order: From Prehuman Times to the French Revolution* (New York: Farrar, Straus and Giroux, 2011), 273.

[5] Francis Fukuyama, *Political Order and Political Decay: From the Industrial Revolution to the Globalization of Democracy* (London: Profile Books, 2015), 206.

[6] Robert D. Woodberry, 'The Missionary Roots of Liberal Democracy', *American Political Science Review* 106, no. 2 (May 2012), 244–74, https://doi.org/10.1017/S0003055412000093.

PRINCIPLE 9: SHARED PRINCIPLES OF EXCELLENCE

ANDREA C. WALDORF

One Christmas Eve in a small city in Central Asia, we cooked something not too strange for our local friends: grilled chicken, boiled rice, and vegetables. Sitting around the *dasdihon* (a tablecloth spread on the floor) a few hours later, our friends diligently moved the food around on their plates; some ate the chicken, but few touched the rest. Losing my patience, I asked, 'Why don't you eat this? It has the same ingredients as a chicken pilau!' Astonished, my friends looked at me and said, 'Yes, but if you knew that, then why did you cook everything separately when it is so much tastier blended together?'

Why indeed? Many of us like to take things apart in our research and analysis. Wanting all the details, we divide our lives and ministries into the secular and the sacred, our work-life balance, word and deed, community development, and church planting. But is the secular not sacred in our hands, our work not part of life? Is not the gospel only whole when heard, seen, and tasted? Is not ministry only whole when we include and integrate all we know, do, and believe?

Our ministry and lives could be tastier to those around us when we live as whole people presenting a whole gospel. A key part of that is to recognise the great compatibility of community development and church planting principles as described in the last two decades.

ACTIVE PARTICIPATION
One of the most important principles in community development today is the active participation of the community in finding solutions and setting the agenda and direction for any development process. This goes back to initial work on participatory rural appraisals (PRA) described by Robert Chambers in his 1983 writings aptly titled *Rural Development: Putting the Last First*.[1]

As pointed out in our earlier article exploring these principles,[2] Chambers' writing on community development issues parallels some of the best thinking in missiology of the time, including the emphases on educational theory and spiritual formation by Ted Ward.[3] Both drew on the pedagogical thinking of Brazilian Paulo Freire,[4] who stressed the importance of the contribution of the local population who can and should be able to analyse their own reality. This concept overlaps with a key principle of Paul Hiebert's description of 'critical contextualization'[5] and many of the principles discussed in the 'vulnerable missions' movement today.[6]

This principle of a deep level of connection to local language and culture has also been discovered in church planting movements (CPM). David Garrison and others emphasise the importance of contextualisation, indigenisation, and evangelism in the heart language of the community as key principles in seeing a CPM happening among those we desire to reach.[7]

Integration into the community in all aspects of life is clearly described in Luke 10, the account of Jesus sending out the seventy-two. He instructs them to stay in the community, live with the people, become part of their life, their joys, their sorrows, their fears and pains, to know what makes them cry or laugh. In other words, he tells his disciples to become neighbours.

Bryant Myers reminds us that to share *our* story, we need to also listen to *their* story. He says,

> '...we face a challenge. How do we merge these stories so that they enhance each other, and everyone learns and grows? The key is becoming community to each other...Building community is what good neighbours do.'[8]

Next, he tells them to deal with the different aspects of life that enable the Kingdom to break into the community through healing the sick (demonstration in the physical realm), proclaiming that the Kingdom is near (proclamation in the intellectual realm), and freeing from demonic oppression (freedom in the unseen spiritual realm). Only in the experience of healing, knowledge, and freedom as a whole can the community understand the fullness of the gospel and embrace it fully. But it is also true that only when the church touches all these areas of life can it be truly vibrant.

REPRODUCIBILITY AND SCALABILITY
Another key principle in community development is reproducibility and scalability. Will your intervention be picked up by the local

Principle 9

community and reproduced locally? Is it simple enough, using locally available resources? Can someone reproduce what you are modelling?

In Central Asia, we designed and locally built assistive devices for children with disabilities, using plastic pipe, wood, and other materials available in the bazaar to build walkers, corner chairs, and other devices. Fathers, grandfathers, and local craftsmen soon came to copy and build their own simple and inexpensive versions for their children or to sell on the local market.

It is the same principle we see in reproducibility and disciple making: We want those we invest in to invest in others and the lessons we taught them to be passed on to others. We want others to look at our friends and say, 'I want what they have: hope for a future, joy in a relationship with God and neighbours, a new centre in life that is infectious.' We want the idea of meeting with others to read God's word to spread from neighbour to neighbour. In a best-case scenario, passing on simple, appropriate technology and sharing the good news go hand-in-hand, truly integral by nature.

In an agriculture project carried out in another community, we provided individual families with a way to grow produce and increase their food security; now the local government has asked us to scale it up for every school in the district. We did not have resources to provide the same technology for all schools, but the project caught others' attention, became a vision that spread and an effective strategy to be adapted and applied elsewhere.

Just as these ideas have been adopted and spread, we want to see groups of people experiencing the vibrancy of a new community of Jesus followers. They in turn will intentionally want to take this to villages and towns that have not yet tasted these good fruits.

COMMUNITY-BASED SERVICES

Further, we should consider the nature of community-based services and how that translates to local churches.

A backbone of community development is the idea that health, rehabilitation, education, and self-help groups (SHGs) are located in direct proximity to the people in need of such services. In this, we speak of primary health versus larger polyclinics in the closest city, village schools established even in remote or nomadic settings, inclusive education for children with disabilities rather than boarding and special education options, and access to legal and peer support through local women's self-help groups rather than isolation.

I sometimes hear the challenge of 'a church in reach of every person'—a community-based church. Johannes Reimer writes that our place of living, our community, is where 'neighbouring' happens and where social networks are formed and maintained. If we want churches to be a transformational power in these networks and communities, they must be part of the community to be 'local'.[9] Yet too many of our churches in the West have become anything but community-based. The idea of a village church—a locally accessible parish—is a dying concept in Europe where many people commute long distances to the church of their flavour. Consequently, the church is no longer physically and socially at the centre of community life or the marketplace. Sad to say, I have seen this as well in some post-Soviet republics, with 'old' churches in the cities expecting believers in the villages to travel to the city, rather than to see a small church planted in the villages.

Although we do not promote this model of large churches, common in our home countries and often featuring 'performance style' worship and 'professional preachers', it is present in the media and accessible to new believers far away. A Central Asian colleague belongs to a small, community-based house church. A year ago, she participated in a financial management course in Germany. While there, she attended a German church with some former colleagues. I picked her up when she returned home. Talking about her trip, she said, 'Finally, I was in a real church; it was like the ones on TV with the music and the preaching.' This broke my heart. I tried to explain that her little group in Asia is also 'real church' and is even more like what the first disciples experienced. She seemed to agree, but I cannot forget that initial heartfelt emotion she showed over attending 'real church'.

As we engage with least-reached communities, let us seek a community-based church model and not repeat the mistakes of the decline of Christianity in our home countries: a church within walking distance, a church for all, a church accessible without a car or funds for local transport, a church where you meet people facing the same struggles as yourself, a church where fellowship continues throughout the week as neighbours interact. Reimer says a missional—we would say a vibrant reproducing—church has an external focus:[10] It looks like its local community; its programmes do not attract into a church building but happen among the people and with the highest level of participation possible.

This church will be a highly participatory and reproducible house church. Apart from such issues as legal registration and buildings, let us consider a *med punkt* (small primary healthcare building) model from the former Soviet Union that was staffed by local communities, within walking distance of the community, and supervised and trained by a regional healthcare worker. Can we imagine churches being at the heart of the village, the marketplace of life, again? Can we imagine our SHGs, farmers' clubs, and parent support groups leading to or becoming vibrant communities of Jesus followers? Can we have spiritual health points overseen by regional apostles in every community?

FOCUS ON GROUPS AND THE EXISTING COMMUNITY—COMMUNITY FORMATION AND TRANSFORMATION

What comes first in the formation of a vibrant community of Jesus followers, the community or the Jesus follower? Community development is based in the community for development of the community. People with a common felt need come together in peer support and problem solving, initially with outside support but focusing on utilising local assets. They form communities to impact their own community. Dave Andrews challenges us as Christian community development workers to practise the principle of community formation since 'Jesus developed an alternative model of community in contrast with the dominant model in the society that he denounced.' Rather than just criticising the injustice of the existing systems, Jesus developed new models. Andrews continues, 'Then Jesus encouraged a movement of people in society who would take the alternatives he had developed with his disciples and implement these principles, practises and processes in their lives individually and collectively.'[11]

Forming a community of new believers from different classes, families, and networks is difficult and often unsuccessful. Community development focuses on key values of community formation, creating networks of trust around common purposes of health, education, agricultural models, non-hierarchical servant leadership, and participatory decision-making that recognises that all are gifted and can contribute. This fresh approach helps us to see biblical aspects of group focus and formation that are not rigidly defined by ethnicity or class—concepts that are important to consider as new communities of believers form.

I was once involved in the set-up of a cooperative for artisans. Our initial employees were widows and other marginalised women of the community. Within a relatively short time, they became a community that looked out for and supported each other, gaining standing in the community both by earning income and enriching their community through tourism.

We prayed for their needs and the business, and we shared our lives. A combination of seeing faith in action, dreams not of Jesus but pointing to 'fruit' in her workplace, and the witness of a local believer led to the first woman coming to faith. Within six months, a large cohort of the workshop had become a community of Jesus followers, reading his word, praying, and supporting each other. It started with community formation, followed by a discipleship of values, integrity, proclamation of the word, and witness falling on fruitful ground where weeds and stones had already been removed by the community itself.

IMPACTING THE WHOLE COMMUNITY

This new community is also the place where wide and relevant seed sowing happens, another principle often quoted in the church planting movement context. Too often when hearing of wide seed sowing, we fall back upon stereotypes of literature and media distribution. These have their place—what is happening these days through social media is amazing—but in our context, the key work is relevant seed sowing into a wide network.

Secular development work often focuses on practical, technical and knowledge solutions. However, in most cultures the underlying question in relation to the development need is often relational and spiritual. As Christians, we can answer the underlying spiritual question of '[w]ho sinned: this man or his parents?' (John 9:2). Sharing development and worldview-relevant good news in community groups and networks helps to identify those who are earnestly seeking God and truth. By sowing relevantly into a wide network of women, farmers, and parents along with the continued watering of these seeds through engagement with the group, those ready for the next step of regularly reading God's word emerge. Interacting with God's word brings a change of worldview and, for some, a change in allegiance and lordship. These changes lead to changed behaviour and lasting transformation in the whole community as a result of obedience to God's word.

SOLIDARITY WITH THOSE WHO SUFFER
'Walking with the poor' and 'putting the last first' are key phrases in the titles of Bryant Myers's and Robert Chambers's great works on community development referenced earlier. There is anecdotal evidence from the recent refugee crises and conflicts in the Middle East that often the forgotten who live in suffering are those responding rapidly to the gospel. At the same time, David Garrison has found a correlation between CPMs and the experience of personal suffering in the workers involved.[12]

Living incarnationally in proximity with the poor and suffering is best demonstrated in Jesus Christ, who was born in poverty, ate and drank with 'untouchables', and was angry with those supporting unjust systems and exploitation. Having an answer—a theology of suffering that holds up not only as we face their suffering but even in our own—is something unique that especially touches the hearts of those who feel forsaken by their god and their own religious brethren.

At the 2018 gathering hosted by the Oxford Centre for Mission Studies giving rise to this book, we discussed a concept since then affirmed by Warrick Farah: Many of the newly emerging church movements have been holistic in nature and naturally contribute to the common good of the community.[13] This seems to be linked at least partly to the more integrated worldview of the national worker and disciple-maker compared to our Western platonic tradition of a divided worldview. Suffering paired with an incarnational, integral mission response through community development and simple acts of mercy is indeed fruitful ground for the emergence of a vibrant church.

In addition, Garrison mentions in his latest book that 'ignored injustices' are a barrier to a church planting movement and conversion. Taking Micah 6:8 seriously to 'act justly, love mercy and walk humbly with our God' is good advice for all of us wanting to reach the least reached.[14]

FOCUS ON TEAMWORK

Finally, the role of intercultural teams is a point of synergy between principles of excellence in community development and the formation of vibrant communities of Jesus followers. More than a decade ago, the development sector addressed what equal participation and inclusion means, both for local community members and Global South staff of NGOs and humanitarian agencies. In the early 2000s, half of my fellow country directors of international NGOs in an Asian network were from the Global South. Between 2010 and 2015, we saw local leadership at the highest national levels in international organisations like Save the Children and Caritas, but many mission organisations lagged behind. Faith-based agencies, once primarily Western in makeup, are finally giving room to our local and Global South brothers and sisters. Some Christian agencies have embraced them for decades but are only now coming to grips with what equal participation and inclusion really mean.

Why is it that those engaged with international development efforts already model some values that the church and those involved in mission among the least reached should deeply believe and readily adopt? These include being diverse and international, giving room to local believers to grow, and as they gain experience, space and opportunity to serve internationally. If mission organisations and churches can become more diverse and empowering—seeing those we disciple as fellow workers in the harvest and as future leaders of communities and organisations—we will have come a long way.

COMPARING PRINCIPLES

Recently, Operation Mobilisation identified ten principles that would help guide us towards fulfilment of our vision 'to see vibrant communities of Jesus followers among the least reached.' In the following table, I compare a brief statement of these principles with its corresponding practice in community development, highlighting how these can reinforce and complement each other.

Principle 9

VCJF principle	Transformational community development context and parallel principle
1. Prayer and fasting	We care for widows and orphans, described as true fasting in Isaiah, and as we engage in transformational development, we need to be aware of the spiritual worldview and powers in the community. (see Chapter 5)
2. Collaboration	We collaborate with the community and all stakeholders. Development should always be an inclusive process.
3. Prepared to suffer	We live among those who suffer and mourn with the mourning, even if this creates risk for us. We seek a theological perspective on suffering together.
4. Do what is easily reproducible	Our development projects are based on local assets and appropriate technology that is reproducible and scalable.
5. Our wide sowing is relevant, contextual, and seeks to elicit a next step	We insert relevant and contextually appropriate spiritual truth in a wide network built through our community involvement.
6. We are in and engaged with the least-reached communities	The least reached are often also least reached in development, education, and economics. Especially in the poorest areas of the world, living in a community as development worker gives us an authentic presence.
7. Form and utilise teams appropriately	Community development is teamwork and already often multicultural and interagency teamwork.
8. Focus on groups	We practise community formation and model healthy communities of peer support and peer learning in our projects.

9. Make disciples, not converts	Community development always views the participants as agents of change, people who hold the potential to change and transform their communities and societies.
10. Local leadership and ownership	Community development is temporary assistance. We model, assist, and lead from the beginning to develop community leaders. As Christian development organisations, we model and teach servant and shepherd leadership to all levels of society.

VCJF Principles and Community Development Practices

All that we have talked about is most clearly defined and distilled in Micah Global's statement on integral mission:

> *Integral mission or holistic transformation is the proclamation and demonstration of the gospel. It is not simply that evangelism and social involvement are to be done alongside each other. Rather, in integral mission our proclamation has social consequences as we call people to love and repentance in all areas of life. And our social involvement has evangelistic consequences as we bear witness to the transforming grace of Jesus Christ.*
>
> *If we ignore the world we betray the word of God, which sends us out to serve the world. If we ignore the word of God we have nothing to bring to the world. Justice and justification by faith, worship and political action, the spiritual and the material,* personal *change and structural change belong together. As in the life of Jesus, being, doing and saying are at the heart of our integral task.*[15]

A BANQUET OF FLAVOURS

A few months ago, I visited a refugee family in a Middle Eastern city, together with a team of our organisation consisting of a Western paediatrician and a Middle Eastern pharmacist. Both spoke Arabic and English well and deeply loved the people they were serving. We visited a family living in utter poverty: the woman was facing difficulties in her marriage and four of her six children had a disability or stigmatising features like albinism. While I observed, the team listened and comforted, gave quality medical advice and referral, and helped the illiterate woman to read medical papers. They shared a lot

Principle 9

of smiles and the two sang a few songs with the children and gave exercises for the girl suspected to have cerebral palsy. Toward the end of our visit, a neighbour came over. My Arab colleague told a story of Jesus, answered more questions, and prayed a blessing on the family. Then we left.

Seldom have I seen all that I have written above lived out in such a small space and time—integral mission lived out and visible in a sixty-minute visit, a banquet of flavours and tastes well blended and pleasing to man and God.

Let us keep together what belongs together; things are tastier when thoroughly blended!

ENDNOTES

---

[1] Robert Chambers, *Rural Development: Putting the Last First* (Burnt Mill, England: Longman Scientific & Technical, 1983).

[2] David Greenlee et al., 'Exploring the Intersection of Community Development, the Least Reached, and Emerging, Vibrant Churches', *Transformation* 37.2 (April 2020), 105-118, https://doi.org/10.1177/0265378819886223.

[3] Duane Elmer, Lois McKinney, and Muriel Elmer (eds), *With an Eye on the Future: Development and Mission in the 21st Century: Essays in Honor of Ted W. Ward* (Monrovia: MARC, 1996).

[4] Paulo Freire, *Pedagogy of the Oppressed* (New York: Continuum, 1986).

[5] Paul G. Hiebert, *Anthropological Insights for Missionaries* (Grand Rapids: Baker, 1985), 171–92.

[6] Alliance for Vulnerable Mission, accessed 19 February 2020, http://www.vulnerablemission.org/.

[7] V. David Garrison, *Church Planting Movements: How God Is Redeeming a Lost World* (Midlothian, VA: WIGTake, 2004), secs 2736, 2756.

[8] Bryant L. Myers, *Walking with the Poor: Principles and Practices of Transformational Development*, Rev. ed. (Maryknoll: Orbis, 2011), 218.

[9] Johannes Reimer, *Die Welt Umarmen: Theologie des Gesellschaftsrelevanten Gemeindebaus*, Transformationsstudien, Bd. 1 (Marburg an der Lahn: Francke, 2009), 253, 254.

[10] Reimer, *Die Welt Umarmen*, 2009, 254.

[11] Dave Andrews, *Compassionate Community Work: An Introductory Course for Christians* (Carlisle: Piquant, 2006), 42.

[12] Garrison, *Church Planting Movements*, 2004, sec. 3784.

[13] Warrick Farah, 'Motus Dei: Disciple-Making Movements and the Mission of God', *Global Missiology* 2, no. 17 (23 January 2020), http://ojs.globalmissiology.org/index.php/english/article/view/2309.

[14] V. David Garrison, *A Wind in the House of Islam: How God Is Drawing Muslims around the World to Faith in Jesus Christ* (Monument, CO: WIGTake, 2014), sec. 3810.

[15] Micah Network, 'Integral Mission', accessed 25 March 2020, https://www.micahnetwork.org/integral-mission.

PRINCIPLE 10:
THE LEAST REACHED ARE SO FOR A REASON

ROSEMARY HACK[1]

I will always remember when I first met *Sally**. Sally is a Malay Muslim; in her country there are severe punishments for both witness and conversion to Christ. However, Sally has further barriers separating her from society: she is transgender and living with HIV. Running and hiding from authorities, it is hard for her to access medical services, or call on police protection. She must avoid the police since being transgender is illegal, and transgender people are frequently subject to harsh beatings by those who should protect them. Who is going to bring the good news of Christ to Sally, stand with her and advocate for her basic rights as a human being created in the image of God?

Entering Sally's world would probably make most of us deeply uncomfortable, having to overcome the usual barriers of access and our own dissonance. Even people from Sally's own culture would discover a wide gap between how they and Sally experience the world around them.

Who will help Sally attain well-being in all aspects of her life? Who will stand alongside her? Even if she were not a Malay Muslim, the chances of her having access to the gospel are slim. It would be fair to say that she is one of the least reached among the least reached.

WHO ARE THE LEAST REACHED?

God created a world that is very good. He is in the business of restoring that creation and bringing justice to those denied it. 'Creation, fall, redemption, consummation—this is the overall structure of the storyline of the Bible.'[2] As followers of Christ, we are a part of this story. If we want the Kingdom of God restored among those least reached by it, then who are we looking to reach and who may we be overlooking?

The least reached have been quantified and identified using complex charts and graphs, divisions of people groups, statistics, and maps. These have proved useful, but in the midst of this sea of data, individuals can become numbers and nameless faces easily overlooked. Seeing people as part of a homogenous group, rather than part of a dynamic community, can mean overlooking some of the least reached. They are the least accessible due to factors such as language, geography, climate, and politics. Their voice is the faintest, marginalised by disability, gender, age, stigma, and shame. Like Sally and her community, least-reached individuals are often embedded in a bigger group that is itself least reached.

The barriers are often ours, not theirs. Stigma is rooted in our hearts; it can cause us to decide who we think is more worthy of our outreach. Often we are more comfortable reaching out to trafficked women than to sex workers or more comfortable helping children with HIV than adults (innocence versus guilt). Jungles or deserts may be their place of comfort; the challenge of living there is ours. Do we present the church in a way that leads nomads to see it as a sedentary institution not suited for those who, as a Somali told Malcolm Hunter, need a church that can go on the back of a camel?[3] The terms we use may become labels—infidel, primitive, native, even 'least reached'—blurring a godly perspective of our common identity with them: made in God's image, potential saints in the Kingdom of God.[4]

As outsiders we sometimes overlook the complexities of religious expression in other societies. Global news coverage has made us aware of the challenges facing the Muslim Rohingya in Buddhist Myanmar. But what of the divisions and prejudices within a broader religious group such as the Shi'a Hazara in Sunni-dominated Afghanistan, the Ismaili sect in Central Asia, or the Sunni Muslim majority under the minority Alawite government of Syria?

In a mountainous setting coloured by such dynamics live a people marginalised not only by climate, geography, and economics but also by their status as a religious minority. Many of them are so poor that they only make it to the market a few times each year. In one of those even less reached villages at the farthest end of a mountain valley, Christian development workers engaged with *Abdul**, helping him build a greenhouse. Abdul loved it so much, he built another with his own resources and now maintains a further two greenhouses that provide vegetables for a school.

Principle 10

Creation is yielding an abundance for this village. Abdul, seeing this, is becoming increasingly aware of God as the creator and sustainer of Earth. Abdul created a resource that benefits his village and allows him to stay there rather than leave his family and migrate for work elsewhere. Development workers have opportunities to pray with him when they visit. With an ongoing relationship and welcome, development workers can worship Jesus in a place where very few Christians have ever set foot.

Recently, people from another village at the end of an even more remote valley came to ask for help to build a greenhouse; the process starts again. Is there a church established in either of these places? No, not yet. The people of these two valleys are still far from being 'reached' but the Kingdom has come, becoming ever more visible.

CHRIST APPEARS ON THE EDGES OF SOCIETY

Jesus grew up in Nazareth, an insignificant town with low social standing (John 1:46). His first followers were from Galilee, at that time a rural crossroads important for its agriculture but looked down upon by religious authorities as a place of impurity and corruption on the periphery of sanctified religion.[5] Jerusalem in the days of Jesus was on the edge of an empire, important as a centre of Jewish identity but not of Roman power and Greek thinking.[6,7] These locations of Jesus' birth, ministry, death, and resurrection were perceived by many as inconsequential.

Many who have yet to encounter Christ also live far from the centres of power, down dirt tracks, beyond the tarmac, in places where it is hard to survive. The 'least reached' are so for reasons both spiritual and often economic in terms of poverty and development. While we do find increasing numbers of 'least reached' congregating in urban settings, focusing on cities is at the cost of those hidden in villages.

Jesus' ministry was not only geographically far from Rome and other centres of power but also far from the people with power, as evidenced by those with whom he often chose to spend time. Prostitutes, lepers, people with disabilities, minority groups such as the Samaritans, or those seen as Roman collaborators such as tax collectors were all on the margins of society, excluded, and stigmatised. Where, in our context, are the people excluded and hidden because of the shame of disability, mental illness, HIV and

AIDS, sexual exploitation and abuse, trafficking, imprisonment, or institutionalisation?

In the mountainous, rural country of Nepal, people living with HIV are highly stigmatised and subject to discrimination. While the country is experiencing dynamic church growth in several regions, people living with HIV are left behind, marginalised and stigmatised even by the church—and by themselves, believing that their ordeal reflects how God feels about them.

Initially, most HIV services were only available in Kathmandu. People living with HIV came to the city for treatment or died in their villages. Many ended up in this large sprawling city with no one to help navigate the hospital system and no accommodation if they were outpatients.

A few followers of Jesus, mostly Nepalis living with HIV, knew the issues and obstacles first-hand. Sacrificing their own time and comfort they stepped into the gap, providing a place to stay and helping new patients at the hospital. However, to serve them better, they needed to get outside of the capital, where 90 per cent of HIV services were concentrated. So they started outposts in a few rural communities many hours of very uncomfortable, dangerous travel away.

Revealing Christ and helping this Nepali community went hand-in-hand. Those living with HIV who contact the ministry know that they are loved, that someone understands and will help them despite their shame and exclusion from society. They know this is because the team is clearly compelled by the love of Christ (2 Cor. 5:14). At monthly support group meetings, Hindus, Muslims, and Christians eat, pray, and worship God together. These gatherings of people from different faiths and people groups are themselves unusual; the fact that they are openly sharing their struggles and requesting prayer adds to the uniqueness of the situation. They have two things in common: HIV and the ministry of those helping them. Many are not yet believers but are on a journey to Christ. The elderly mother of one client recently was baptised and started to follow Jesus. Her son was asked if he was a believer; his answer, 'Not yet!', came with a smile and the implication that it is only a matter of time.

Principle 10

RURAL DEVELOPMENT TOURISM

In his ground-breaking work of the early 1980s, Robert Chambers wrote that the underserved are so because they are unobserved; they are not along the 'rural development tourism' route.[8] Many of his concepts transfer readily to missiological issues. The least served and least reached are indeed not along the 'rural development tourism route' or, in our terms, the 'short-term missions tourism route'. Chambers goes on to say, '[I]n aid agency parlance "the field" now usually means the receiving country which in turn usually means the capital city...Where there is a security problem, the hold of the capital city is even more severe.'[9]

The least reached may be in far flung places, such as those behind a barrier of snow in the Himalayas, or closer to home. In some cases, it is not a geographic barrier but a curtain of shame that renders people invisible.

Often people with disabilities are least-reached because they, or those caring for them, are afraid and ashamed of the stigma associated with disability. Working with people with disabilities is a practical way to demonstrate their worth, opening a door for people to understand that they are loved both by God and by those who serve them.

The elderly is another group often hidden from our view, a cluster of less reached among the least reached. A profound experience changed the thinking of a colleague working among refugees:

> *Every time I drove to the refugee camp, I would see an old lady sitting beside the highway. This went on for weeks until I finally listened to the prompting of the Spirit who said: 'Do you see her? I see her. Stop for her.'*
>
> *One day I did, and it was a paradigm-shifting experience. I encountered her as Jesus to me—very humbling, sharing our humanity and honouring her for who she was. I didn't verbally share the gospel with her, but I believe I definitely demonstrated the gospel to her. I truly encountered Jesus in her, the least of these. Maybe the least reached are more reached than we think, and we need to be touched in fresh ways by Jesus in them.*

In the encounter with this elderly woman, my colleague encountered a humbling truth: Among the least reached we ourselves may find our own 'least reachedness', our own need of ongoing change, and an opportunity to learn from those the world considers weak.

NO HEROES NEEDED

Many studies have firmly established the principle that the most effective outreach and community development work are done bottom-up not top-down.[10] In our efforts to help people, we need to come alongside as humble servants, empowering them to become all that Christ would have them to be. Japanese theologian Kosuke Koyama observes, 'Too often Christianity exhibits a "crusading mind" rather than a "crucified mind" and...suffers from a "teacher complex".'[11] We must resist the temptation to act or speak in ways that imply that we have all the answers and have come to save people from their ignorance. Indeed, in many such situations we are the ignorant. Cultural and linguistic differences are another reason people are not reached and the message is misunderstood.

Robert Chambers[12] referred to barriers separating community development workers from underserved, impoverished[13] populations. Among these is the wide divergence between the culture of the impoverished community and that of the development workers, or of the different nature and content of their knowledge. Assumptions are made about one (possibly similar) community that are not true about another more impoverished community.

In some situations there may not be any same-culture, or even near-culture Jesus followers. However, just as the local community should be the true owners of the community development effort, where there are local Jesus followers, it is key that they are part of the process, being listened to and either taking the lead or being equipped to do so in the future.

How can this bottom-up, near-culture approach contribute to transformation? In Myanmar, local believing families and teams are moving into underdeveloped, isolated rural villages to incarnate Christ among those who have had no gospel witness. By living in these communities, the village teams understand local needs such as addressing domestic violence, HIV, and substance abuse. Together with the community, they address these issues through the training and expertise of networks in their city-based support team.

Principle 10

THE POWER OF PRESENCE

In 1956 Jim Elliot, Roger Youderian, Ed McCully, Pete Fleming, and Nate Saint attempted to reach the Waorani (commonly known as 'Aucas') of Ecuador's eastern jungles. When the five were found dead on a remote river beach, the news flashed around the world. Many years later Bonnie Witherall was assassinated in a clinic in Lebanon where, compelled by the love of Christ, she served women and children. News of her sacrifice also flashed around the world. Over the years many others have also given and risked their lives because of a passion to see people come to know Christ.

There are still people today entirely without a human witness to Christ, some also without a digital witness. However, in this internet age, could not most of those who do not know Jesus find the truth if they looked for it? Perhaps, if truth were in words alone. But truth is embodied in the person of Christ and is to be lived out. Miroslav Volf speaks of truth in Ephesians 4:15 as a verb: 'Commentators usually render this term "speaking the truth in love." But the verb used in the original is not "to speak" but "to truth"'. It is something that you do and live out, both telling and living.[14]

The scriptures tell us that we are known by our love, a signpost pointing to God. But it will take more than being physically present to reach people. This is where community development and living the love of Christ unite with lasting impact. Community development is not a platform to gain access to people nor something that we can sever from the verbal proclamation of the gospel of the Kingdom that touches the physical, spiritual, mental, and emotional. It is not 'pie in the sky when we die' but real life, abundant life, right here, right now.

As Rizalina Ababa (Chapter 3), Gabriel Markus (Chapter 4), and Mark Galpin (Chapter 7) discussed, community development without the spiritual basis is not transformational as it fails to address the whole person. As Christians, we would add that it restores *shalom* to the community. True *shalom* is a restoration of broken relationships: peace with God, peace with one's self, with others, and the environment.[15] The Kingdom of God alone brings the spiritual transformation which is missing from secular programmes.

In identifying who is not being reached, we begin with the end in mind. As Christopher Sugden wrote, 'The end of development...its true identity, [is] the restored identity of the poor as "children of

God with a gift to share.'"[16] If this restored identity is part of the goal of development, how much more as Christians must we seek out neglected communities that lack *shalom* and are clearly in need of Christ?

LENSES AND ASSUMPTIONS
People can be 'least reached' because Jesus followers are not part of their community—or because Jesus followers fail to see them in their own community. Lenses help us to focus our vision; depending on the lens chosen, we may have a broad field of view or one filtering out all but certain features. A lens to see things far away may leave us blind to what is at our feet.

Some lenses used to view the priority task of the Church are driven by demographic data and projections about those who have heard—or are presumed to be likely to hear—the good news. The right lenses might help us confirm where those least-reached with the gospel overlap with the communities most in need of development, or with areas where the impact of environmental degradation is strong.

But seeing from a distance, even with a powerful lens, is not enough. To know who is truly least-reached both in community development and evangelism terms, we need to walk the streets and interact with people. A community development lens may help us see obvious and not so obvious issues of material or social poverty and also implications of what people might or might not know about Jesus.

In the United Kingdom's inner cities, underprivileged communities are populated with people trapped in generational poverty and are characterised by addiction, abuse, underachievement, and hopelessness. Parents and children slip through systems meant to help them. Isolated from the gospel message, they would never darken the doors of largely middle-class British churches[17] whose growth is mostly from immigrant and black majority communities.[18]

The Message, a Christian charity, is focused on reaching the bottom 10% of society, people who are among the least reached in the United Kingdom. Starting in 1988 with a large evangelistic outreach, an estimated 20,000 young people heard the gospel message. However, in 1996, after seeing that many of the young

Principle 10

people who trusted in Christ did not know how to live out their newfound faith, the charity started thinking more holistically.

Benchill, in Manchester, was at that time the most deprived neighbourhood in the UK. The Message had a vision to see Christians moving into areas like Benchill to live and work, building community, seeing neighbourhoods transform. Andy Hawthorne, founder and CEO of The Message explains, 'A driving philosophy was that the ministry should be characterised both by social justice and unashamed gospel proclamation, embodying what Jesus called "salt" and "yeast" and "a lamp on a stand"' (Matt. 5:13–16; 13:33).[19]

The work expanded into prisons, and soon men and women from highly dysfunctional backgrounds were finding new life in Christ. However, in too many cases they were leaving prison with little or no support. Something new was needed: a combination of a supportive, mentoring community, decent housing, and a way of providing employment for those who had often fallen out of the system at a young age. Work began on developing training and jobs in various viable businesses. The re-offence rate is minimal, far below the national rate of 47%,[20] and the vibrancy of faith is palpable.

Gary Bishop describes how he heard the call. 'I had never been to Manchester before I came to my interview,' he says. 'I was overwhelmed. It was tipping with rain and this building was in a bit of a state—brown on the outside, paint peeling off, graffiti…I went back and said to Hannah [now his wife]: "I don't care if I never go back there again."'[21] But he did go back and has seen transformation in the community.

ALL THE EASY PLACES ARE TAKEN

Proactively reaching the least reached—people that others have given up on—will take us out of our comfort zones. Rebecca spoke of this 'not giving up' attitude in describing her challenging work with street children in Africa.

> *Secular organisations believe that if a child is on the street more than a year, they are hopeless to be helped and changed. I have known children who were on the street more than a year and God has changed their lives. John* was an addict and alcoholic living on the streets for many years. He started attending a Christian programme where he heard the gospel and accepted Jesus. Even though change came, there were times that he backslid, but he was able to*

repent and keep trying to follow God. Today he is following Jesus, living with his wife and family, and working as a mechanic.

This could also mean going far out of our comfort zones to areas that remain unreached because of conflict, war, terrorism, danger, and restrictive governments making access harder. Robert Chambers mentions a bias of development workers to areas that are more secure.

This (security bias) is probably becoming more important in development work. Considerations of security discourage or exclude visits to areas where the visitor might not be safe. The cumulative effect of this exclusion is that visitors lack experience of being personally insecure, and may fail to appreciate what physical insecurity means to many poor people and the priority many accord to peace and civil order.[22]

Sue Arnold, discussing the balance between risk and compassion, sums up this perspective:

All the easy places are taken...Reaching them (the unreached) will not be easy for a variety of reasons: persecution from governments, hostility from locals, dangerous roads, wars, politics, local crime, terrorism, or extreme weather (just to name a few).[23]

And yet we must hold this perspective of risk with humility and nuance. While risk may be involved in serving the least reached, among them we may find a warm welcome and sense of home. Rather than physical risk, for some the risk may be more of exposing and opening ourselves to those we perceive to be different to us, including the alien and sojourner living nearby.

OPENED DOORS, PLEASANT SURPRISES

In their Introduction, the editors of this book told of a development team in a conservative Muslim area in rural Central Asia, no easy place to serve. Their community development work among children with disabilities was the door-opener to relationships, which came to be greatly appreciated by the community. At a recent community event, a local government official thanked the team for coming to take care of their children, something he admitted that they themselves had neglected.

Principle 10

Sue Arnold[24] talks about 'balancing risk vs. counting the cost.' Putting people (or oneself) at risk is a difficult decision not to be taken lightly. If we want to reach the least reached, we have to consider this with wisdom and boldness for the sake of the gospel.

In the Kurdish region of northern Iraq, a team has access to refugees and internally displaced people due to war. This door opened through permission to work with people with disabilities, distributing much needed wheelchairs and conducting other 'tent visits' to serve and bring practical help and hope. It was not merely permission, though; the relationships developed because some were willing to go and be a loving, caring presence in this high risk and isolated region.

The least reached are often hidden, separated not just from us but also from their own society by hostile environments, danger, disease, gender, stigma, poverty, and complex webs of sin. They are hidden at times by our own blindness or simply our failure to observe with Spirit-enabled perception. When we make the extra intentional effort to find, come alongside, understand, and serve them we may find ourselves in places where we are not expected, in the words of Bryant Myers,[25] a 'pleasant surprise' that may open hearts and minds to the service and love Christ compels us to offer.

ENDNOTES

---

[1] I am thankful for the significant collaboration of a friend with long experience in community development work. For privacy reasons she remains unnamed.

[2] Steven C. Roy, 'Embracing Social Justice: Reflections from the Storyline of Scripture', *Trinity Journal* 30 NS (2009), 3.

[3] Malcolm Hunter, 'Foreword', in David J. Phillips, *Peoples on the Move: Introducing the Nomads of the World* (Carlisle: Piquant, 2001), xiii.

[4] Paul G. Hiebert, *The Gospel in Human Contexts: Anthropological Explorations for Contemporary Missions* (Grand Rapids: Baker Academic, 2009), 191.

[5] Orlando E Costas, *Liberating News: A Theology of Contextual Evangelization* (Eugene: Wipf & Stock, 2002), 51.

[6] E. Randolph Richards and Brandon J. O'Brien, *Misreading Scripture with Western Eyes: Removing Cultural Blinders to Better Understand the Bible* (Downers Grove: IVP Books, 2012), 65.

[7] Eckhard J. Schnabel, *Early Christian Mission: Jesus and the Twelve*, vol. 1 (Downers Grove: InterVarsity, 2004), 197.

[8] Robert Chambers, *Rural Development: Putting the Last First* (Burnt Mill, England: Longman Scientific & Technical, 1983), 10–11.

[9] Robert Chambers, 'Poverty Unperceived: Traps, Biases and Agenda' (IDS Working Paper 270, Institute of Development Studies, 2006), 9, 10.

[10] See, for example, Nigel Scott et al., 'An Evidence-Based Study of the Impact of Church and Community Mobilization in Tanzania' (London: Tearfund, 2014).

[11] Cathy Ross, 'The Theology of Partnership', *International Bulletin of Missionary Research* vol. 34 (2010), 147.

[12] Chambers, *Rural Development*, 1983.

[13] Impoverished in the broad sense of the word, not just monetary poverty, as later described in Christian, *God of the Empty-Handed*, 2011.

[14] Miroslav Volf, *Exclusion and Embrace: A Theological Exploration of Identity, Otherness, and Reconciliation* (Nashville: Abingdon, 1996), 256.

[15] Bryant L. Myers, *Walking with the Poor: Principles and Practices of Transformational Development*, Rev. ed. (Maryknoll: Orbis, 2011), 144.

[16] Christopher Sugden, *Social Gospel or No Gospel?*, 2nd rev. ed. (Cambridge: Grove Books, 1977), 144.

[17] Madeleine Davies, 'Class Divide at Church Must Be Addressed, New Study Suggests', *Church Times* (4 August 2017), https://www.churchtimes.co.uk/articles/2017/4-august/news/uk/class-divide-at-church-must-be-addressed-suggests-new-study.

[18] Rhiannon McAleer, 'Church Growth: The Numbers', *Transmission* (Spring 2018).

[19] Andy Hawthorne, *Here I Am: Joining God's Adventurous Call to Love the World* (Colorado Springs: David C Cook, 2019).

[20] 'Prison: The Facts' (Prison Reform Trust, 2013), http://www.prisonreformtrust.org.uk/Portals/0/Documents/Prisonthefacts.pdf.

[21] Guardian Staff, 'A Choice in the Wilderness', *The Guardian* (2 November 2005), sec. Society, https://www.theguardian.com/society/2005/nov/02/socialexclusion.guardiansocietysupplement.

[22] Robert Chambers, *Poverty Unperceived: Traps, Biases and Agenda* (Brighton: Institute of Development Studies, 2006), 32, https://opendocs.ids.ac.uk/opendocs/bitstream/handle/20.500.12413/665/Wp270%20web.pdf?sequence=1&isAllowed=y.

[23] Sue Arnold, 'The Risk of Reaching the Unreached: Finding the Balance between Safety and Compassion', *Lausanne Global Analysis* (10 September 2019), https://www.lausanne.org/content/lga/2019-09/risk-reaching-unreached.

[24] Arnold, 'The Risk of Reaching the Unreached', 2019.

[25] Personal conversation, Bryant Myers with David Greenlee, June 2018.

SERVING THE LEAST REACHED THROUGH COMMUNITY DEVELOPMENT: A PERSONAL JOURNEY OF UNDERSTANDING

A COMMUNITY DEVELOPMENT WORKER IN ASIA

Why are people 'least reached'? Our definition of the term, explored briefly in the Introduction, is drawn in part from Colossians 1:6—they have not heard and understood the gospel in all its truth. Is it just that they have not heard the words and ideas, or is it that they have not seen it through our actions? And who are 'they'? What are the barriers that keep people 'out of reach'? Is it somehow their fault or sin or religion, is it the fault of history and borders and wars, or is it somehow related to me and my own perceptions?

My own journey of understanding began in South Africa, growing up in an unjust system of racism. God was calling me to go where the needs were the greatest. For me that meant moving out of my comfort zones of the city to areas where unemployment, migrant labour, and racial discrimination led to shacks being built at the edges of larger cities. In these 'townships' and 'squatter camps', I met with people with disabilities, though often we were not able to travel to these areas because of protests or threats to our own safety.

SEEING BEHIND THE MAP
God was challenging me personally to go where both physical and spiritual needs were the greatest. I started learning about the interaction of these basic needs when I moved to work in Southeast Asia. Prior to this I had been impacted by maps of major world religions—the 'unreached' in the so-called '10/40 Window'. I learned that Buddhism was one of the major religions in this area. However, actually living there revealed many other factors at play in making this one of the harder to reach places.

The area where I worked was a day's drive away from the capital, driving through winding jungle roads. From there it was another one-hour trip, sitting on a small wooden bench in the back of a van, crossing an army checkpoint—all to reach displaced people living in the border areas who, unable to return to their country due to civil war and ethnic fighting, were not welcomed into the country they were fleeing to. Geography, hard to access jungle terrain, physical access, political unrest, and ethnicity were all at play in putting these people further out of reach.

ZEROING IN ON HUMAN NEED

God helped me zero in on more needs beyond this. I was asked to help at a safe house run by a couple—both of them followers of Jesus from the local community—situated in the jungle just outside a major refugee camp. This safe house took in those from the refugee camp or surrounding jungle areas who were unable to care for themselves due to disability, mental illness (sometimes through the stress of fleeing the fighting), injuries, HIV, or simply old age.

The needs were great. I was very humbled that in these circumstances God did not need my pride in my professional background, ability, or knowledge. I was humbled by my inability to meet these many needs and also by the love and care that the local Christian couple and other volunteers showed these people. I came face to face with those who would otherwise be forgotten, overlooked, or even die if not cared for. This spiritual experience was like zooming in on a Google map from the world religious 'blocs', through jungles and remote towns to those people who might be forgotten or unnoticed. Zooming in on human need allowed me to see how disability, mental illness, physical illness or injury, old age, and physical displacement from fleeing unrest interact to categorise these people as the least reached.

Riding a motorbike with a local co-worker along a muddy track through rice paddies and jungle one day, we came to the bamboo hut of a young man from an ethnic minority. Paralysed in an accident, he had lost his job and therefore his income. We sat and talked with him and his wife, who cared for him daily. Sitting at their bedside, sharing words of faith, hope, and comfort while showing practical ways to make caring easier, I realised that these are the people who are isolated, hidden, and harder to access.

THEIR WELCOME IMPACTS MY LIFE

My journey of discovery continues in Central Asia. For a number of years I have been working in Central Asia, living in a rural area a long day's drive from the capital on steep, winding, and bumpy roads through stark mountain scenery. I live in an area where the post-Soviet borders on the map have been drawn in strange squiggly lines.

From the town where I live, it is another one-hour trip in a crammed minibus along a road dotted with military checkpoints to a town even more cut off by the mountainous terrain where we visit people with disabilities. I call on a home where a *bibi* (grandmother) carries her disabled granddaughter on her back because of lack of access to a wheelchair in addition to narrow steps that lead up the steep path to their house. This girl has no access to schooling; very few people would know that she is housebound with her elderly grandparents. Against this backdrop are the larger issues of post-Soviet Islam: the conservative dress codes, headscarves, and small community mosques where men go to pray on Fridays. Here, political unrest, remoteness, and conservative Islam are in stark contrast to the warmness of the welcome. 'Come in and drink a cup of tea with us,' they say as we are welcomed into a simple room with floor mats.

What would I have missed out on in my life if I had not taken the step to come here? The privilege of getting to know these people and the beauty of the culture and warm hospitality that has impacted me and left footprints on the landscape of my life. Before moving to this part of the world, my own fears could have held me back. Very real thoughts of not raising enough finances, of war in a neighbouring country or what it means to live among Muslims led to fear of risk or insecurity that I had to work through. Maybe it is often our own views or prejudices of Islam or perceived danger that are the real barriers to us going to the least reached.

WHERE PHYSICAL AND SPIRITUAL NEEDS INTERTWINE

Reflecting on factors that make people least-reached, we must consider where the hidden and hard places are in the world. I have been impacted with maps like the '10/40 Window' and the startling statistics on people groups with no believers or witness. I read about millions living in poverty and unemployment or children who die daily from preventable diseases. These extreme physical and spiritual needs meet on a global scale; in these contexts we see individuals with unmet physical and spiritual needs. If we choose to ignore disability, disease, street children, refugees, or migrants, then we will continue to leave large pockets of society unreached. Beyond global statistics and labels of 'religion', 'Muslim world', or 'Asia' for example, we can zoom into the reality of broken and difficult circumstances where physical and spiritual needs intertwine.

Of course, deep human need exists in big cities, not just in remote areas, and it exists in my home city in South Africa, not just in Central Asia. In South Africa there are enough churches that I would assume that there are at least some followers of Jesus, including in those areas of need, who might respond and share the fulness of the gospel. But here in Central Asia—although mothers and fathers love their children, and there are some in the community who want to help—who is there who can point them to Jesus and the beauty of the gospel message that can bring transformation to their lives?

LEARNING FROM THE LEAST REACHED

Another factor that I face daily in my work among children with disabilities in Central Asia is the barrier of stigma and belief systems. Beyond traditional Islamic practices, 'folk Islam' sees physical problems as having spiritual roots for which solutions are sought through mullahs, spiritists, fortune tellers, rituals, and amulets.

Working with children with disabilities in this environment has taught me a lot. Mothers share with me their beliefs that perhaps their child is cursed, or their own sins are being punished through the disability of their child. They ask me, 'What did I do wrong that God is punishing me in this way?' Such parents will naturally hide their child and the shame of being seen as punished, rejected, or cursed by God.

Children with disabilities are often hidden from society by stigma and beliefs isolating them and their families. This physical need interacts with belief systems, and stigma and isolation follow. Another perspective is that this is all pre-ordained; your fate (*nasib*) is written on your forehead at birth. Whatever happens to you is purely fate; God himself is distant or does not care. If this is so, why would one want to relate to such a God?

SURPRISING PRESENCE

In this environment we have a community-based rehabilitation project, where mothers can bring their children with disabilities twice a week. One mother remembers walking into the room and feeling an atmosphere of kindness and love never before experienced when people saw her severely disabled daughter. Through practical rehabilitation, exercises, and the child playing in the group, we and the family noticed much progress.

This mother met with other mothers in similar situations, breaking through the isolation and shame. I could share how God loves her and her child, that the God I believe in is a God of love who would not curse a child with a disability; rather, he wants to reach out in love and forgiveness. There are many opportunities to pray with mothers—both for their child and also for God to show his love to them. It is here where the tangible experience of being loved interacts with the message of a loving God.

This mother is now no longer shy to take her daughter out on the street or in a minibus. Recently at a training event for mothers of children with disabilities, she shared what she had heard from us: God is a loving father who will not give us a stone if we ask for bread when we ask him to help us in our circumstances. The reality of this message is passed on, even while this mother still processes her understanding about God.

In this context, where less than one per cent of the population are believers, our community-based rehabilitation and development approach has given us access to many homes in remote villages. In these conservative Islamic areas, we are welcomed; suspicion is removed as they learn we are here to help them and their disabled children. In a government speech at one of our events, we were thanked for helping those whom they themselves as Muslims had not been willing or able to help. I have come across this 'surprise' in people we interact with here: 'Why would you come to this area so rural and difficult to work with people that we see as having no value?'

I sometimes also get the opposite reaction: 'What you are doing is really good work that pleases God.' Traditional Muslim belief holds that a person's good and bad deeds are weighed on a balance on the Day of Judgment; if you have more good deeds than bad you will have at least a good chance to enter paradise. In their minds, then, our good works help us earn 'points' towards salvation (*kori savob*). When people comment on our good works, we have the ideal opportunity to talk about salvation, sin, grace, and how good works alone cannot save us.

Working here for a number of years, we have seen many families change their perspective towards disability, as many children show improvement. We have also had many conversations about God and spirituality. A few, interested to hear more, have started reading the Bible. This is the road of a long-term relational presence in an area that is seen as 'hard ground' where we walk with people in difficult situations until the truth of a loving God can be fully understood by them.

SERVING THEM IN LOVE
Community development helps us find the hidden and needy people, enter hard to reach places, and break down resistance; it comes with a message of compassion for the lost through showing real care for them. Community development gives us strategies to help remove the 'us–them' barrier by working in ways that do not create dependency but trust. For many in these contexts, disability is a spiritual issue at its root cause. Addressing it with love is the spiritual response that people seek, opening opportunities for further conversations.

When I think of the least reached, I think of the disabled girl crying in a dark room because her mother is hiding her from shame; the deaf girl in a village where no one can communicate with her or has ever taught her sign language; the man crawling towards me in the dust in front of his house because he has no wheelchair and his world ends at his gate. As far as I know there are no followers of Jesus among these, the least of the least reached. Precious women, children, and men, they are made in the image of God. We will serve them and thus serve the God who, without distinction, loves us all.

EPILOGUE: CALLED TO UNDIVIDED WITNESS

PAUL BENDOR-SAMUEL

What, then, is the relationship between community development and the emergence of vibrant communities of Jesus followers among people who are least reached with the gospel of the Kingdom? This is a vitally important question for all those who believe both that there is no other name by which we can be saved and that God's salvation includes the reconciliation and renewal of the whole of creation. The answers turn out to be complex, unpredictable, varied, sometimes very tough, yet filled with joyful surprise. Our understanding of the nature of God's mission, his Kingdom, and how people enter that Kingdom makes a difference. Since opposition to the gracious rule of God is evident at personal, interpersonal, and systemic levels in society, every part of this ministry is concerned with a cosmic fight for the freedom of the children of God and the renewal of all creation. It is ministry in and through the power of the Spirit. We can identify principles to guide our thinking and praxis, yet there is no formula or recipe for success in this kind of integrated ministry.

The consultation at the Oxford Centre for Mission Studies in October 2018 that led to this book brought together a group eager to tell their stories of what they had seen and experienced. From their research and reflection, a number of themes emerged. The principles outlined in this book are not simply theoretical ideas drawn from community and church development literature; they arise from reflection on the lived experience of mature intercultural workers. There is a richness in what they share. Here I simply want to draw upon three areas that may help us understand better the work of God's Spirit at the nexus of material and spiritual need among the least reached.

OUR NEED TO LISTEN CLOSELY

History is told by the powerful, and much mission history has been no different. However, since the 1990s, increasing attention has been paid in mission literature to hearing the voices of those served by the Protestant intercultural mission movement. A beautiful example of this is the personal story behind Chapter 4: Gabby Markus' journey of service from his home in Papua New Guinea to tsunami relief coordination in Sri Lanka and, at the time of writing, helping coordinate the response to refugees in Greece by the evangelical churches there.

Some of our authors speak from their own contexts, such as Sally Ababa from the Philippines. The shift to recording mission history from the perspective of local participants has yielded some surprising results. One key insight has been that, far from being passive recipients of the gospel from those more powerful than they, local evangelists and disciplers have been the primary means for the spread of the gospel.

When it comes to understanding what is going on in a community, whether intrapersonally, interpersonally, or within a group, we need to hear the voices of the primary actors: the people of the local community. The authors of this book are seasoned intercultural workers who demonstrate the importance of paying close attention to the voices in their communities. We can only make sense of what we observe and feel, and what we observe and feel is shaped by our biases, some that we are aware of, many that we are not. These biases are not necessarily right or wrong; they simply 'are'. Assumptions, experience, culture, gender, age—the list of things that determine what we 'see' and experience is long. So strong are our subconscious filters and biases that 'we do not think and talk about what we see but we see what we are able to think and talk about.'[1] The challenge remains in mission research to hear directly the beliefs, experiences, self-reflection, and sense-making of those among whom God is at work. We have made a good start in this book.

Furthermore, the contributors to this volume have avoided language that objectifies people or that suggests they are a target of our vocation or expertise. Why is this so important? In part, it is because such labelling makes it more difficult for us to see those we serve as genuine partners in development and discipleship. Any form of labelling risks creating categories of 'us' and 'them' rather than 'we'. Genuine listening demands a posture of respect, curiosity, and openness. In addition, labelling in mission (using terms like 'unreached' or 'people groups') can feed into a bigger narrative of what has been described as mission-by-management. In subtle

Epilogue

ways, we begin to see mission as a task, dependent on technique, strategy, speed, and scale rather than on relationship, vulnerability, listening, and dependence on God.

This leads to a second area of need; our need to see clearly.

OUR NEED TO SEE CLEARLY

Who are least reached people today? Boundaries that hinder the flow of the good news of the Kingdom may be ethno-linguistic, the classic assumption of unreached people group categorisation. This volume demonstrates that least-reached communities defy stereotyping. They may be people living in remote valleys in mountainous Central Asia but could just as easily be slum dwellers in a city bustling with lively middle-class churches.

As explained in the Introduction, the 'least reached' no longer exist primarily in neat, geographically located 'people group' clusters. Not only are they dispersed widely through migration and urbanisation, vast numbers of least-reached communities are found in contexts where the church exists, and may even be strong, yet these communities remain distant to the gospel due to all kinds of frontiers, many of which are now primarily intellectual, social, and ethical.

Todays' least reached are not living only in remote places. They may be in front of our eyes, but because of our mission paradigm and the language we use, we simply don't see them, as Rosemary Hack points out in Chapter 10. Take as an example the impact of rapid urbanisation. Today over 30 per cent of all those who live in cities inhabit slums—an estimated 1.3 billion people.[2] While accurate figures are difficult to obtain, in 2014 Todd Johnson and his colleagues estimated that fewer than 1 in 500 Christian foreign missionaries are working in slums, 1 in 10,000 national workers works in slums in their own countries, and the vast majority of these missionaries and workers live outside the slums.[3] Could it also be that it is not only our language of mission that hides the neediest from our sight but also our relative power and wealth?

OUR NEED TO ASK HUMBLY

The need to hear and see in different ways leads us to an underlying posture of a humble learner. This posture underpins each of the ten principles we have explored in this book. Humble learning requires new skills and particularly the ability to move from telling to asking.

When we move into intercultural ministry we come sincerely, even as servants, but, sadly, we so often come assuming we have the answers. The world of community development has long taught us that there is no transformation without participation; and participation means much more than merely going along with what those from outside the community propose. Andrea Waldorf, exploring Principle 9, reminds us of the many ways excellent community development can inform the way we share the good news of the Kingdom. Some of us come from cultures that overvalue telling at the expense of asking. Edgar Schein, renowned organisational development expert, writes about this in his helpful little book *Humble Inquiry*: 'I now realise that the issue of asking versus telling is really a fundamental issue in human relations and that it applies to all of us all the time.[4]

Schein points out that when we tell someone something, we establish ourselves in the position of power. In contrast, when we genuinely ask questions for which we do not have answers, we humble ourselves and empower the other, placing ourselves at that moment in a place of dependence. Our voluntary subordination creates psychological safety for the other. This here-and-now humility, as he puts it, can help modify the status and power that come through colour, ethnicity, language, gender, education, and wealth. Such a posture builds trust and relationship, especially across cultures. Schein calls this genuine asking 'humble inquiry'. Reading the stories retold in these pages beautifully illustrates time and again this gracious posture.

Humble inquiry is only effective when we recognise our ignorance and that our best attempts to understand the other are seen through the lenses of our filters and biases. Humble inquiry underpins appropriate, sustainable development but also effective witness to Christ as we seek to discover what the other believes and experiences of God. It underpins effective contextual discipleship, which asks, 'What does it mean to follow Jesus here?' Humble inquiry insists on hearing the voices of those we seek to serve, positioning us to bear witness to Christ, who is able to meet their needs.

Epilogue

Flowing from the faith, hope, and love that characterise Christian discipleship, humble inquiry is a foundational posture for those who work among the poor and marginalised and who long to see the Kingdom come and God's will done for them. It helps us to hear better and see more clearly. It is a foundational posture in those who seek to understand more deeply the relationships between community development and the growth of vibrant communities of Jesus followers in communities where the good news of the Kingdom is least seen and heard.

LEARNING IN NORTH AFRICA: A PERSONAL EXPERIENCE

Those invited by God to participate in integral ministry on the margins of gospel witness find it a place of deep personal learning and growth, a journey of discipleship. That was certainly what my wife and I experienced during the twelve years we spent working in North Africa in the interface between community development and growth of communities of Jesus followers. A story comes to mind from those days:

> *I was called to travel from the capital to a remote province where one of our teams had been working for about five years. In the previous two years, a small group of Jesus followers had grown from the witness of one man whose life had been transformed. Caught with his hand in the finances where he worked, he was staggered when his boss, one of our team, forgave him and gave him an opportunity to change. His response was to request a copy of 'our book'. Who was this Jesus who could make a person behave so differently from what most bosses would do? It was the beginning of a transforming process, an encounter with Christ that changed him, his wife, and his family, and then began to ripple out to others in the community. After some months, the police decided enough was enough and the group was shut down.*

> *This was not the end of the matter. The Regional Director of Health, my closest personal friend in the country, was scandalised, incensed. 'What inducements did you give to persuade him to change his religion? You have corrupted our culture.' Very quickly the Ministry of Health withdrew from all our projects, leaving the future of the organisation hanging in the balance. So it was that I found myself driving to a meeting with the provincial governor, with no idea what I would say. I walked into his large office and was graciously received. 'Your Excellency,' I started, 'you have known that we are Christians, supported by churches. We have always given our very best professionally, seeking to serve with integrity. The motivation that drives the excellence of our professional work flows from our experience of the love*

of God. This same motivation means that when someone asks us about our faith, we have to share about that love we have freely received. We respect that this is your country and you have the right to invite us to stay or ask us to leave. However, we are whole people, and you cannot split us in two. You cannot have professional excellence without a willingness to share what makes us who we are.' Very graciously, His Excellency shook my hand and asked us to stay.

CALLED TO UNDIVIDED WITNESS

Whole people or not at all. This challenge is not for those we go to, as if we have some right to lay down conditions for service and proclamation. No, this challenge faces each of us as we seek to bear faithful witness to the God of creation and recreation, of life and new life, of relationship and reconciliation. Anything less is a betrayal of the God who took on our materiality in the incarnation and in so doing announced the arrival of the Kingdom and the renewal of all things under the gracious lordship of King Jesus. God is calling us to bear undivided witness—whole people with a gloriously whole gospel. What a calling!

ENDNOTES

[1] Edgar H. Schein, *Humble Inquiry: The Gentle Art of Asking Instead of Telling* (San Francisco: Berrett-Koehler, 2013), 91.
[2] Gina A. Zurlo, Todd M. Johnson, and Peter F. Crossing, 'Christianity 2020: Ongoing Shift to the Global South', *International Bulletin of Mission Research* 44, no. 1 (January 2020), 8–19, https://doi.org/10.1177/2396939318804771.
[3] 'Christianity in Its Global Context, 1970–2020: Society, Religion, and Mission' (South Hamilton, MA: Center for the Study of Global Christianity, 2013), 85.
[4] Schein, *Humble Inquiry*, 2013, 4.

Contributors

Rizalina (Sally) Ababa received an MA in Sustainable Development, MA in Religious Education, and MDiv. Born and raised in the Philippines, she has been involved in community work since her high school days and has served with Operation Mobilisation since 1997, including as National Director in the Philippines from 2013–2020.

Martin Allaby (PhD) chairs the Faith and Public Integrity Network. He has 10 years' experience in community and public health in South Asia and has researched the response of Christians to corruption across Africa, Asia, and Latin America. He works as a doctor for the National Institute for Health and Care Excellence in England.

Paul Bendor-Samuel (MD) is Executive Director of the Oxford Centre for Mission Studies. Trained as a medical doctor, he and his wife spent 12 years in North Africa working in primary healthcare and community development followed by 12 years leading the international ministry of Interserve. His research interests include the realignment of the intercultural mission movement and the development of spiritually healthy organisations.

Scott Breslin (EdD) is a senior advisor in conflict resolution at the Nordic School of Management and has more than 25 years' experience in consulting and project management in Europe, Central Asia, and the Middle East. Scott's doctorate in education is from the University of Edinburgh.

Mark Galpin (PhD) is Postgraduate Programme Leader at All Nations Christian College and lecturer in poverty and justice studies. He has 30 years' experience of community development in South Asia and Africa and worked most recently as the Executive Director of United Mission to Nepal.

David Greenlee (PhD), raised in Colombia, is a missiologist who has served since 1977 with Operation Mobilisation and, for the past 20 years, as Director, Missiological Research and Evaluation.

Rosemary Hack has a background in fashion design. She joined Operation Mobilisation in 1979 and with her husband has ministered in various places around the world (Middle East, Asia, Africa). Passionate about issues of injustice and oppression, she founded AIDSLink International in 2006.

Gabriel (Gabby) Markus is from Papua New Guinea and holds an MA in Development and Missions. After living in Nepal and Myanmar, he served in Sri Lanka for four years as Programme Manager during the 2004 tsunami relief effort. He has lived in Greece since 2012, working with refugees, the homeless, and victims of human trafficking.

Robert Sluka (PhD) leads A Rocha's Marine and Coastal Conservation Programme (www.arocha.org/marine) and has worked cross-culturally, living for extended periods in Australia, Maldives, India, Great Britain, and his native USA where he currently resides.

Holly Steward has a BA in English and Music and a background in HR management. For nine years, she lived in a remote part of northern Zambia, leading a team of Zambians and working in an orphan school and a medical clinic. She serves on the Global Board for OM International.

Andrea C. Waldorf (MSc Global Health) has been involved in community development work in Central Asia since 1996. In 2008 she became country director for her organisation and since 2018 has served as Associate International Director for Programme Development.

Jonathan Williams has lived and worked with rural communities in Southeast Africa and Central Asia. He has provided project support to a large international Christian organisation, including capacity building in holistic development and participatory development approaches. Jonathan has undergraduate qualifications in Agriculture with Environmental Management, as well as postgraduate studies in Managing Rural Development.

FOR FURTHER READING

The following list includes many of the resources referred to by our authors. Where reference has been made to a chapter in an edited volume, we list here the entire book. Rather than include complex URLs, items labelled (Internet) can be readily found using appropriate search terms taken from the title and author.

COMMUNITY DEVELOPMENT: GENERAL READING
- Béné, Christophe, Andrew Newsham, Mark Davies, Martina Ulrichs, and Rachel Godfrey-Wood. 'Resilience, Poverty and Development.' *Journal of International Development* 26, 5 (2014): 598–623. (Internet)
- Chambers, Robert. 'Reflections and Directions: A Personal Note.' *PLA*, Critical reflections, future directions, 50 (October 2004), 23–34. (Internet)
- Chambers, Robert. 'Poverty Unperceived: Traps, Biases and Agenda.' IDS Working Paper 270: Institute of Development Studies, 2006. (Internet)
- CHS Alliance. 'Core Humanitarian Standard on Quality and Accountability' (2014). (Internet)
- Giordano Quintana, Christian. *Bibliografía comentada de desarrollo* [Annotated bibliography of development]. Santander: Misiopedia.com, 2013. (Internet)
- Ledwith, Margaret. *Community Development: A Critical Approach*, 2nd ed. Bristol: Policy Press, 2011.
- Sato, Turid, and William E. Smith. 'The New Development Paradigm: Organizing for Implementation.' In *Development: New Paradigms and Principles for the Twenty-First Century (Rethinking Bretton Woods)*, Vol. 2. Eds. Jo Marie Griesgraber and Bernhard G. Gunter. London: Pluto Press, 1996. (Internet)
- Schein, Edgar H. *Humble Inquiry: The Gentle Art of Asking Instead of Telling*. San Francisco: Berrett-Koehler, 2013.
- Sen, Amartya. *Development as Freedom*. Oxford: Oxford University Press, 2001.

- Walker, Peter, and Catherine Russ. 'Professionalising the Humanitarian Sector.' London: ELHRA, 2010. (Internet)
- Community Development Exchange. 'What Is Community Development?'. (Internet)

COMMUNITY DEVELOPMENT: PERSPECTIVES OF CHRISTIAN WRITERS

- Andrews, Dave. *Compassionate Community Work: An Introductory Course for Christians.* Carlisle: Piquant, 2006.
- Chester, Tim. *Good News to the Poor: Sharing the Gospel through Social Involvement.* Leicester: Inter-Varsity Press, 2004.
- Chester, Tim. *Is Everything Mission?* Nottingham: Keswick Ministries, 2019.
- Christian, Jayakumar. *God of the Empty-Handed: Poverty, Power, and the Kingdom of God,* 2nd Kindle. Victoria, Australia: Acorn Press, 2011.
- Corbett, Steve, and Brian Fikkert. *When Helping Hurts: How to Alleviate Poverty without Hurting the Poor – and Yourself,* New ed. Chicago: Moody, 2012.
- Giordano Quintana, Christian. 'En busca de una misiología integral: las relaciones entre proyectos de desarrollo iberoamericanos no proselitistas en tierras musulmanas y las iglesias pioneras vinculadas a ellos'. PhD dissertation. Vrije Universiteit, 2020. (Internet)
- Global Development Practitioners. *Hands: Stories and Lessons of Wholistic Development.* Colorado Springs: CAMA Services, 2019.
- Greenlee, David, Mark Galpin, Andrea Christel, and Cameron Willett. 'Exploring the Intersection of Community Development, the Least Reached, and Emerging, Vibrant Churches.' *Transformation* 37, no. 2 (April 2020), 105-118.
- Kusch, Andreas, Ed. *Transformierender Glaube, Erneuerte Kultur, Sozioökonomische Entwicklung: Missiologische Beiträge zu einer Transformativen Entwicklungspraxis.* Korntaler Reihe, Bd. 5. Nürnberg: VTR, 2007.
- Mitchell, Bob. *Faith-Based Development: How Christian Organizations Can Make a Difference.* Maryknoll: Orbis, 2017.

- Myers, Bryant L. *Walking with the Poor: Principles and Practices of Transformational Development*, Rev. ed. Maryknoll: Orbis, 2011.
- Scott, Nigel, A. Foley, C. Dejean, A. Brooks, and Simon Batchelor. 'An Evidence-Based Study of the Impact of Church and Community Mobilization in Tanzania.' London: Tearfund, 2014. (Internet)
- Shah, Rebecca Samuel, and Joel Carpenter, Eds. *Christianity in India: Conversion, Community Development, and Religious Freedom*. Minneapolis: Fortress, 2018.

CREATION CARE

- Bell, Colin, and Robert S. White, Eds. *Creation Care and the Gospel: Reconsidering the Mission of the Church*. Peabody, MA: Hendrickson Publishers, 2016.
- Bookless, Dave. 'Context or Content? The Place of the Natural Environment in World Mission'. In *Missional Conversations: A Dialogue between Theory and Praxis in World Mission*, Eds. Cathy Ross and Colin Graham Smith. London: SCM Press, 2018.
- Bookless, Dave. *Planetwise*. Nottingham: IVP, 2008.
- Cracknell, Deborah. *By the Sea: The Therapeutic Benefits of Being in, on and by the Water*. London: Aster, 2019.
- Halapua, Winston. *Waves of God's Embrace: Sacred Perspectives from the Ocean*. Norwich: Canterbury, 2008.
- Nichols, Wallace J., and Celine Cousteau. *Blue Mind: The Surprising Science That Shows How Being near, in, on, or under Water Can Make You Happier, Healthier, More Connected and Better at What You Do*. London: Back Bay Books, 2015.
- Sluka, Robert D., Martin Kaonga, Janice Weatherley, Vijay Anand, Daryl Bou, and Colin Jackson. 'Christians, Biodiversity Conservation and Poverty Alleviation: A Potential Synergy?' *Biodiversity* 12.2 (2011), 1–8. (Internet)
- Sorley, Craig. 'Christ, Creation Stewardship, and Missions: How Discipleship into a Biblical Worldview on Environmental Stewardship Can Transform People and Their Land.' *International Bulletin of Mission Research* 35 (2011), 137–43.

MISSIOLOGICAL REFERENCE

- Arnold, Sue. 'The Risk of Reaching the Unreached: Finding the Balance between Safety and Compassion.' *Lausanne Global Analysis* (10 September 2019). (Internet)
- Boorse, Dorothy. *Loving the Least of These*. Washington, DC: National Association of Evangelicals, 2011. (Internet)
- Breistein, Ingunn Folkestad. 'Missionary Activities and Human Rights: Recommended Ground Rules for Missionary Activities'. Oslo Coalition on Freedom of Religion or Belief, 2009. (Internet)
- Farah, Warrick. 'Motus Dei: Disciple-Making Movements and the Mission of God.' *Global Missiology* 2, no. 17 (23 January 2020). (Internet)
- Galpin, Mark. *Living in God's Story: Understanding the Bible's Grand Narrative*. United Kingdom: Micah im:press, 2018.
- Hyam, Matt. *Life before Death: A Study of Judgment and Eternal Life in John's Gospel*. Southampton: Hopeful Ink, 2018.
- Lim, David Sun. 'From Asia: Education for Economic Transformation.' *William Carey International Development Journal* (5 October 2017). (Internet)
- Maggay, Melba Padilla. 'Integral Mission: What's It All About?' In *Integral Mission Training Module*. Pasig City, Philippines: Institute for Studies in Asian Church and Culture, 2008. (Internet)
- Maggay, Melba Padilla. *Transforming Society*. Eugene: Wipf & Stock, 2011.
- Micah Network. 'Declaration on Integral Mission' (27 September 2001). (Internet)
- Padilla, C René. 'What Is Integral Mission?' *Del Camino Network for Integral Mission in Latin America*. (Internet)
- Padilla, René, Melba Maggay, and David Westlake. 'Basic Introduction to Integral Mission.' *Micah Network Integral Mission Initiative*. (Internet)
- Morphew, Derek. *Breakthrough: Discovering the Kingdom*, 5th ed. Cape Town: Vineyard International, 2019.
- Ramachandra, Vinoth. 'What Is Integral Mission?' *Micah Network Integral Mission Initiative*. (Internet)

Further Reading

- Reimer, Johannes. *Die Welt Umarmen: Theologie des Gesellschaftsrelevanten Gemeindebaus*. Transformationsstudien, Bd. 1. Marburg an der Lahn: Francke, 2009.
- Reimer, Johannes. *Missio Politica: The Mission of Church and Politics*. Carlisle: Langham, 2017.
- Samuel, Vinay and Chris Sugden, Eds. *Mission as Transformation: A Theology of the Whole Gospel*. Oxford: Regnum, 1999.
- Thacker, Justin. 'A Holistic Gospel: Some Biblical, Historical and Ethical Considerations.' *Evangelical Review of Theology* 33, no. 3 (July 2009).
- Thiessen, Elmer. *The Ethics of Evangelism: A Philosophical Defence of Ethical Proselytizing and Persuasion*. Milton Keynes: Paternoster, 2011.
- Wanak, Lee, Ed. *The Church and Poverty in Asia*. Mandaluyong City, Philippines: OMF Literature, 2008. (Internet)
- World Council of Churches, Pontifical Council for Interreligious Dialogue, and World Evangelical Alliance. 'Christian Witness in a Multi-Religious World: Recommendations for Conduct' (2011). (Internet)
- Wright, Christopher J. H. *The Mission of God: Unlocking the Bible's Grand Narrative*. Downers Grove: IVP Academic, 2006.
- Wright, N.T. 'Tom'. *Surprised by Hope*. London: SPCK, 2007

GENERAL INDEX

1910 World Missionary Conference, 57

A Rocha, 11, 84–85, 88, 91
Afghanistan, 144
Agriculture, 21, 105, 133, 135, 145
Aid, 40, 60, 66–67, 101, 110–115, 118–119, 147
AIDS (see 'HIV and AIDS')
Andrews, Dave, 135
Arnold, Sue, 152–153
Asian Theological Seminary, 46
Athens, Greece, 56, 62
Australia, 84–85

Balance, 16, 26, 44, 48, 101, 126, 132, 152 155
Banda Aceh, Indonesia, 39–40
Baptism, 38, 57, 146
Batak tribe, 47–48
Bauckham, Richard, 92
Bible (see also 'Word of God'), 15, 21, 25, 30, 34, 37–38, 43–45, 48, 56–57, 61, 63, 75, 77, 85, 123–124, 126–128, 143, 162
Bishop, Gary, 151
Blessing, 18, 84, 104–106
Bookless, Dave, 91
Boorse, Dorothy, 88
Buddhism, 35, 157

Cairo, Egypt, 105
Calleja, Rachael, 112
Cape Town Commitment, 67–68, 83
Caritas, 138
CDLR space, 3–4, 6–8, 91
Cebu City, Philippines, 43, 45
Central Asia, 1, 8, 11, 28, 36, 40, 65, 78–79, 111, 131, 133–134, 144, 152, 158, 160, 165
Chambers, Robert, 113, 131, 137, 147–148, 152
Change, 4, 6–7, 9, 11, 16, 25–26, 29, 38, 40, 45–46, 51, 63, 65, 71–72, 75, 80–81, 92, 98–100, 104–105, 107, 140, 151, 162, 167
  agents of change, 100, 140
  individual change, 1, 41, 45–46, 51, 62–63, 65, 68, 71, 99–100, 106, 137
  structural change, 46, 99–100, 106, 140
  worldview change, 99, 137
Children (see also, disabilities, children with), 25–26, 33, 39, 43–45, 47, 68, 72–73, 97, 144, 149, 150–151, 159, 160
Christian, Jayakumar, 26, 29–30, 79
'Christian Witness in a Multi-Religious World', 68
CHS Alliance, 113
Church, churches, 1–2, 6–7, 19, 21, 28–30, 33, 38, 41, 43, 45–52, 56–62, 67, 71, 77, 83, 85, 88, 98, 102, 104, 106, 126, 128, 132–138, 144–146, 150
Church planting, 3, 12, 41, 97–98, 131–132
Church planting movements, 132, 136–137
Cities (see 'urban settings')
Climate change, 44, 84
Community development (see also 'development'), 1–8, 10–12, 15–19, 22, 27, 29–30, 39, 41, 46, 48, 55, 60, 72, 79–80, 83, 86, 88, 91–92, 97–100, 102–106, 109, 111, 114, 120, 123, 131–133, 135, 137–140, 148–150, 152, 162–163, 166–167
  defined, 4–5
  practitioners, workers, 1–4, 6, 15, 18, 22, 24–25, 28–37, 40, 44, 46, 55, 61, 78, 80, 86–88, 101, 109, 111–115, 118, 120, 126, 135, 137, 139, 145, 148, 152
Community, communities (see also 'health, community'), 1–2, 4–12, 16–18, 21–22, 24–26, 28–30, 36, 39–41, 45, 47–49, 51, 55, 59–60, 65, 71,

73, 75–76, 80, 83, 85–89, 97–98, 100–105, 110, 114, 119, 126, 131–140, 144, 146, 148–152, 158, 160–161, 163–165, 167
Compassion, 15, 25, 36, 44, 50, 58, 61, 152, 162
Conduct, codes of, 68, 113
Consultation on the Church in Response to Human Need, 98
Conversion(s) (see also 'coming to faith', 'Kingdom of God, entering'), 33, 36, 50, 68, 99, 103, 106, 137, 143, 167
Corbett, Steve, 49
Corruption, 11, 44, 79, 80, 111, 118, 123–128
Creation, 15, 17, 22, 26, 44, 59, 62, 78, 83–86, 88, 92–93, 104, 143, 145, 163, 168
new creation, 26, 85, 92–93
Creation care, 11, 17, 83–93, 173
Cross (of Jesus), 34, 62, 85, 93,
Culture, cultural, 1, 5, 8, 47, 49, 51, 59, 80, 84, 89, 99, 126, 132, 136, 143, 148, 159, 164, 166–167
intercultural, 138, 163–164, 166
multicultural, 51, 139

Daoism, 35
Darfur, Sudan, 110–111
Das, Rupen, 50
Deliverance, 24, 74, 79, 81
Demon, demoniic 27–28, 72, 74, 80, 132
Dependence, dependency, 18, 39, 49, 71, 162, 165–166
Development (see also 'community development', 'transformational development'), 2–3, 5–8, 19, 26, 28–30, 40, 49, 52, 86–88, 99, 101, 110, 113–114, 131, 136, 139, 145, 147, 149–150, 152, 161, 164, 166
Christian perspectives, 9, 26, 50, 88, 98–100, 106, 110
faith-based, 7, 40–41, 120
goal of, 9, 24, 26, 85–86,104, 150
Devil (see 'demon, demonic')

Disabilities, 1, 6, 78–79, 144–145, 147, 158–159, 162
children with, 1, 78–79, 133, 140, 152, 160–161
people with, 45, 145, 147, 153, 157, 159
Discipleship, disciple making, 18, 36, 51, 71, 89, 99, 103, 106, 133, 136–138, 140, 164, 166–167
Discovery Bible Study, 1
Donor(s), 66, 109, 112–113, 120
Dreams, 1, 74, 136

Ecuador, 45, 58, 149
Edinburgh, Scotland, 57–58
Education, educational, 5, 43, 47, 71, 75, 79, 97, 124, 126, 132–133, 135, 139, 166
Edwards, Michael, 110
Egypt, 105
Empowerment, 4–5, 18, 21, 24, 39, 135, 138, 148, 166
England (see also, 'United Kingdom'), 125
Ethics, 10–11, 18, 39, 65–69, 101, 114, 126, 165
Evangelism, evangelise (see also, 'ethics'), 2, 7, 10, 12, 33–34, 44–46, 48, 50–51, 55–56, 58–59, 62, 65–69, 98, 100–103, 106, 112–113, 132, 140, 150,

Faith-based organisations (FBOs), 2, 7, 18, 40, 101–102, 109, 112–113, 115, 119–120, 138,
Family, families, 1, 44, 71–73, 78–79, 97, 119, 133, 135, 140–141, 145, 148, 152, 160–162, 167
Farmers, farmland, farms, 21, 45, 85, 118, 135–136
Fasting, 17, 74, 79, 139,
Fernando, Ajith, 65
Fikkert, Brian, 49
Food, 55–56, 61–62, 71, 74, 83–84, 131
food security, 97, 133
Forgiveness, 28, 34, 37, 44, 50, 77, 161

General Index

Freedom, 8, 11, 15, 28, 39, 57, 66, 68, 73, 77–78, 97, 132, 163
Freire, Paulo, 132

Galatsi, Greece, 56
Garrison, David, 132, 137
Germany, 134
Giordano, Christian, 3
Global South, 50, 138
Godwin, Roy, 104–105
Good News (see 'gospel'), 7, 33–35, 39, 47, 60, 68, 73, 91–92, 133, 136, 143, 150, 165–167
   'Good News' (fishing boat), 75–76
Gospel, 5, 16, 18, 22 24–26, 29, 33, 37, 44, 47, 50–51, 58, 60, 63, 65–69, 76–77, 83, 91–92, 102–104, 131–132, 137, 140, 143, 147–151
   Gospels, gospel accounts, 27–28, 35, 37, 98
'Grand Rapids Report', 58
Great Reversal, the, 49
Greece (and 2015-16 refugee crisis), 10, 55–57, 60–61, 67, 164
Green Desert Project, 92
Gulrajani, Nilimia, 112

Halapua, Winston, 90
Hawthorne, Andy, 151
Healing, 22, 24, 26–27, 30, 56, 71, 105, 132, 135
Health, 38, 90, 97, 101, 102, 111, 124, 127, 133
Health care, healthcare, 71–72, 135
Hiebert, Paul, 35–36, 99, 132
Hindus and Hinduism, 21, 24, 34, 41, 146
HIV and AIDS, 33, 36, 44, 143–146, 148, 158
Holism, holistic, (see also 'transformation, holistic'), 9, 12, 29, 45–47, 49, 50, 59, 63, 65, 69, 86, 89, 92, 98, 106, 137, 140, 151
Holy Spirit, 17, 24–27, 29–30, 37, 62, 73–74, 76, 79, 99–100, 105–106, 147, 153, 163

Honour, dishonour, 34–35, 39, 116–117, 128, 147,
Hope, 16, 33, 36, 49, 66, 75, 80, 85, 92–93, 102, 104, 106, 133, 153, 158, 167
   hopeless, 28, 71, 73, 150–151,
   proximate and ultimate hope, 92
Hunter, Malcolm, 144
Hyam, Matt, 25

Identity, 6, 15, 25–26, 47, 66, 68, 90, 99, 101, 104, 144–145, 149–150
Impurity (see also 'purity'), 34, 145
Indian Ocean, 89
Indonesia, 39, 76, 89
Injustice (see also 'justice'), 28, 79, 123–124, 135, 137
Integral mission, 10, 16, 44–47, 50–52, 58–59, 65, 67, 89, 98, 137, 140–141
Integrity, 63, 65, 101, 126, 128, 136, 167
Iraq, 153
Isidro, Gadiel, 47
Islam (see also 'Muslims'), 57, 88, 112, 159–161

Jones, Howard, 33
Justice (see also 'injustice'), 16–17, 45–46, 51, 58, 100–101, 123–124, 140, 143, 151

Kathmandu, Nepal, 146
Kenya, 88–89
Kingdom of God, 10, 12, 15–17, 22–30, 33, 36–38, 41, 47, 51, 56, 59–60, 62–63, 65, 73, 80–81, 83, 85–86, 92, 97, 123, 127, 132, 143–145, 149, 163
Ko, Lawrence, 92, 95
Koning, Otto, 76–77
Koyama, Kosuke, 148
Kreider, Alan, 1–2

Labels, labelling, 59, 154, 160, 164
Lake Tanganyika, 71, 73–75, 77
Latin America (see also 'South America'), 3, 45, 49

179

Latin American Theological Fraternity, 45, 58
Lausanne Covenant, 58
Lausanne Movement (see also 'Cape Town Commitment,' 'Consultation on the Church in Response to Human Need,' 'Grand Rapids Report,' 'Lausanne Covenant'), 83
Lebanon, 149
Ledwith, Margaret, 99
Liberation, 26
Liberation theology, 48–49
Lim, David, 39, 51, 66
Livingstone, David, 71, 77
Luther, Martin, 118, 127

Maggay, Melba, 51, 59, 98–99, 103
Malaysia, 89
Manchester, England, 151
Manila, Philippines, 46
Message, messages, 66, 77, 101, 106, 148
  gospel message, 2, 10, 24–25, 29, 44, 50, 56, 59, 69, 119–120, 150, 151, 160–162
  Message, the (charity), 150–151
'Micah Declaration', 45
Micah Global, Micah Network, 58–59, 98, 140
Middle East, 8, 111, 137, 140
Mindanao, Philippines, 43
Mitchell, Bob, 7, 40, 99, 101
Moffitt, Bob, 43, 52
Mongolia, 92–93
Morphew, Derek, 23
Movement, movements (see also 'church planting movements'), 6–7, 21, 30, 51, 98, 125, 132, 135, 137, 163
Muslims, 1, 3, 34, 38, 41, 78, 83, 143–144, 146, 152, 159–161
Myanmar, 144, 148
Myers, Bryant, 2, 7, 9, 24–25, 98–99, 132, 137, 153

Nepal, 67, 146
Niamey, Niger, 40

North Africa, 3, 167

Oceans, 89–91

Padilla, C. René, 45–46, 58–59
Palawan, Philippines, 47–48
Papua, Indonesia, 76
Papua New Guinea, 164
Peace, 25–26, 34, 51, 57, 74, 103, 124, 149, 152
Peace, Richard, 33
Persecution, 21, 101, 126, 152
Philippines, the, 10, 43, 47, 51, 89, 164
Polynesia, 90
Poor, the, 2, 15, 21, 24–30, 40, 46–47, 49–50, 73, 79, 87–88, 99, 116, 120, 123–124, 137, 139, 144, 149, 152, 167
Poverty, 4–6, 8–9, 11, 16, 19, 22, 24, 27–28, 44, 47–49, 56, 79, 99, 105, 137, 140, 145, 153
  poverty alleviation, 2, 27, 49, 86, 88, 117, 124
Power, powerful (see also 'empowerment'), 11, 26, 39, 72, 80–81, 124–128, 134, 145, 149, 163–166
  powerless, powerlessness, 26, 29, 39, 79
  spiritual power, 22–24, 26, 29–30, 51, 62, 71, 74–81, 103, 106, 139, 163
Practitioners (see 'community development, practitioners, workers')
Prayer, 15, 17, 24, 30, 34, 72–75, 77–79, 92–93, 105–106, 117–118, 139, 146
Priority, 44, 55, 57–58, 109, 150, 152
Professional excellence, 11, 18, 91–92, 109–117, 120, 167–168
Proselytism, 51, 66–68, 97, 101, 112, 119–120

Ramachandra, Vinoth, 65
Reformation, the, 46–47
Reimer, Johannes, 103, 134

General Index

Rejoicing, 76–77, 80–81
Relief, 2, 4–5, 10, 27, 41, 55–56, 60, 67, 164
Repent, repentance, 36–37, 46, 50, 75–77, 140, 152
Reproducibility, 18, 132–135, 139
Resilience, 4, 87–88
Ringma, Charles, 46
Risk, 4, 66, 112, 114, 124, 139, 149, 152–153, 159, 164
Rohingya, 144
Russ, Catherine, 113

Sahara, 89
Salvation, 25, 49, 56, 58–60, 65, 78, 80–81, 161, 163
Save the Children, 138
Schein, Edgar, 166
Sen, Amartya, 8
Senegal, 3
Servant, 125, 135, 140, 148, 166
Serve, service, 1, 6, 8, 10–12, 16–19, 24, 30, 37, 40, 45–46, 51, 55–56, 58–63, 65–67, 69, 72, 76, 84–85, 88, 92–93, 97, 101, 103, 105, 112, 117–119, 138, 140, 146–147, 149, 152–153, 162–164, 166–168
Services, 62, 90, 110, 124, 133, 143, 146,
Shalom, 9–11, 15, 25, 28, 30, 104–105, 149–150
Signs of the Kingdom, 16, 26, 28, 62–63
South Africa, 11, 77, 128, 157, 160
South America, 88
South Asia, 8, 98
Southeast Asia, 8, 11, 33, 89, 91, 157
Spiritual warfare, spiritual battle, 17, 28, 71–81, 92,
Sri Lanka, 10, 35, 41, 55, 60–61, 65, 164
Stigma, 140, 144–147, 153, 160
Sudan, 110–111
Suffering (see also 'persecution'), 2, 16, 18, 29–30, 60–62, 65– 66, 77–78, 91–92, 109–111, 116–118, 137, 139, 148,
Sugden, Christopher, 149

Supernatural signs (see also 'deliverance', 'dreams', 'healing'), 1, 24, 26
Switzerland, 38
Syria, 144

Team, teams, 1, 28–29, 33, 35, 38, 48, 56–57, 71–72, 74–75, 77, 83–84, 91, 97, 101–103, 138–140, 146, 148, 152–153, 167
Teamwork, 18, 138–139
Tertullian, 2
Thacker, Justin, 59
Thiessen, Elmer, 68
Thomas, I'Ching, 35
Train, training, 1, 18, 21, 29, 45, 48, 52, 89, 91, 106, 110, 113, 135, 148, 151, 161
Transformation, 9–11, 15–18, 30, 39, 44, 49, 73, 77, 97–100, 102, 104–106, 134, 137
  and blessing, 104
  defined, 100
  goal of, 26
  holistic transformation, 16–18, 29, 45, 47, 98, 140
  personal transformation, 16, 33, 45, 49, 76, 99, 103–104, 106
  transformative change, 6, 12, 72, 99
Transformational development, 2, 7, 26, 46–47, 52, 104, 139
Trust, 15, 41, 65, 75, 111, 124, 135, 162, 166
Tsunami, (2004 Boxing Day), 10, 40–41, 55, 61, 65, 88, 104, 164
Tutu, Desmond, 128

United Kingdom, 99, 150
United Nations, 111
'Universal Declaration of Human Rights', 102
Unreached, 2, 5, 29–30, 152
Urban settings, 38, 40, 90, 134, 145, 150, 157, 160, 165
Urbanisation, 90, 165

Vibrant communites of Jesus
  followers (VCJF), 6–7, 10–12, 15,
  17–18, 22, 29, 55, 88–89, 91–92, 97,
  100, 104–106, 135, 138–140, 163,
  167
Volf, Miroslav, 149

Wales, 105
Walker, Peter, 113
Ward, Ted, 132
West Africa, 38
Wheaton Declaration, 58
Wink, Walter, 79–80
Word of God (see also 'Bible'), 22,
  46–47, 140

World Evangelical Alliance, 59, 83
World Health Organization (WHO),
  111
Worldview, 44, 50, 85, 91, 99–100,
  136–137, 139
Worship, 2, 17, 22, 46–47, 59, 61–63,
  71, 76–78, 93, 119, 134, 140, 145–
  146,
Wright, Christopher J. H., 22, 60, 62,
  104
Wright, N.T. 'Tom', 25, 29

Zambia, 11, 71, 73, 75, 77, 80
Zurich, Switzerland, 38

Scripture Index

Genesis 1:1, 84
Genesis 2:15, 85

Exodus 15:18, 23

Deuteronomy 28:8, 105

Psalm 33:6, 9, 10-11, 22-3
Psalm 82:4, 79
Psalm 100, 61
Psalm 139:23-24, 115

Proverbs 14:31, 116
Proverbs 31:8-9, 116

Isaiah 6:5, 34
Isaiah 10:1-3, 123
Isaiah 43:6-7, 61
Isaiah 58, 17, 79
Isaiah 58:10, 79
Isaiah 61:1-3, 73

Jeremiah 29:7, 17

Micah 6:8, 137
Micah 7:3, 123

Matthew 4:4, 49
Matthew 5:13-16, 151
Matthew 5:14-16, 73
Matthew 5:16, 116, 120
Matthew 5:17, 47
Matthew 6:10, 51
Matthew 6:11, 117, 120
Matthew 7:21-23, 37
Matthew 10:23, 23
Matthew 12:28, 23
Matthew 13:33, 151
Matthew 16:18, 47
Matthew 17:2, 98
Matthew 19:26, 37

Matthew 25:1-13, 23
Matthew 23:23, 45
Matthew 25:35-36, 44
Matthew 28:18-20, 17

Mark 1:15, 23
Mark 9:2, 98
Mark 10:15, 37
Mark 10:17-22, 37
Mark 16:15, 85

Luke 4:18-19, 47, 73
Luke 7:22, 73
Luke 11:42, 45
Luke 12:11-27, 23
Luke 13:22-30, 37
Luke 15:19, 34
Luke 17:20-21, 23
Luke 19:10, 47
Luke 21:32, 23
Luke 24:27, 26

John 1:46, 145
John 3:3, 37
John 3:16, 25, 37
John 4:35-38, 55
John 5:37, 39, 47
John 6:66, 39
John 8:36, 64
John 9:2, 136
John 10:10, 9
John 13:34-35, 2

Acts 3:19, 36
Acts 26:20, 36

Romans 5:19, 9
Romans 8:17, 80
Romans 8:37, 73
Romans 9:33, 34
Romans 10:13, 60

Romans 12:2, 98

2 Corinthians 3:18, 99
2 Corinthians 5:14, 146
2 Corinthians 5:18, 9
2 Corinthians 5:18-20, 119, 120
2 Corinthians 5:19, 44

Ephesians 2:10, 117
Ephesians 2:14-18, 9
Ephesians 3:10, 80
Ephesians 4:15, 149
Ephesians 6:7-8, 119
Ephesians 6:12, 72, 81

Philippians 2:5-11, 34

Colossians 1:6, 157
Colossians 1:12-14, 37
Colossians 1:15-20, 9
Colossians 1:20, 85
Colossians 3:23, 119

1 Timothy 4:8, 56

2 Timothy 2:12, 80

Hebrews 4:12, 77
Hebrews 11, 81

James 1:2-4, 76
James 1:27, 116

1 Peter 2:9, 120
1 Peter 2:12, 2
1 Peter 2:24, 34
1 Peter 3:15, 16, 60, 66, 102, 106, 108

1 John 1:9, 34, 35
1 John 4:18, 72

Revelation 5, 85
Revelation 5:9-13, 93
Revelation 5:13, 85
Revelation 12:10-12, 81
Revelation 21, 22, 9
Revelation 21:4, 9